2-14-05	DATE DUE		
FE 28 '05			
MR 02 '05			

North Carolina

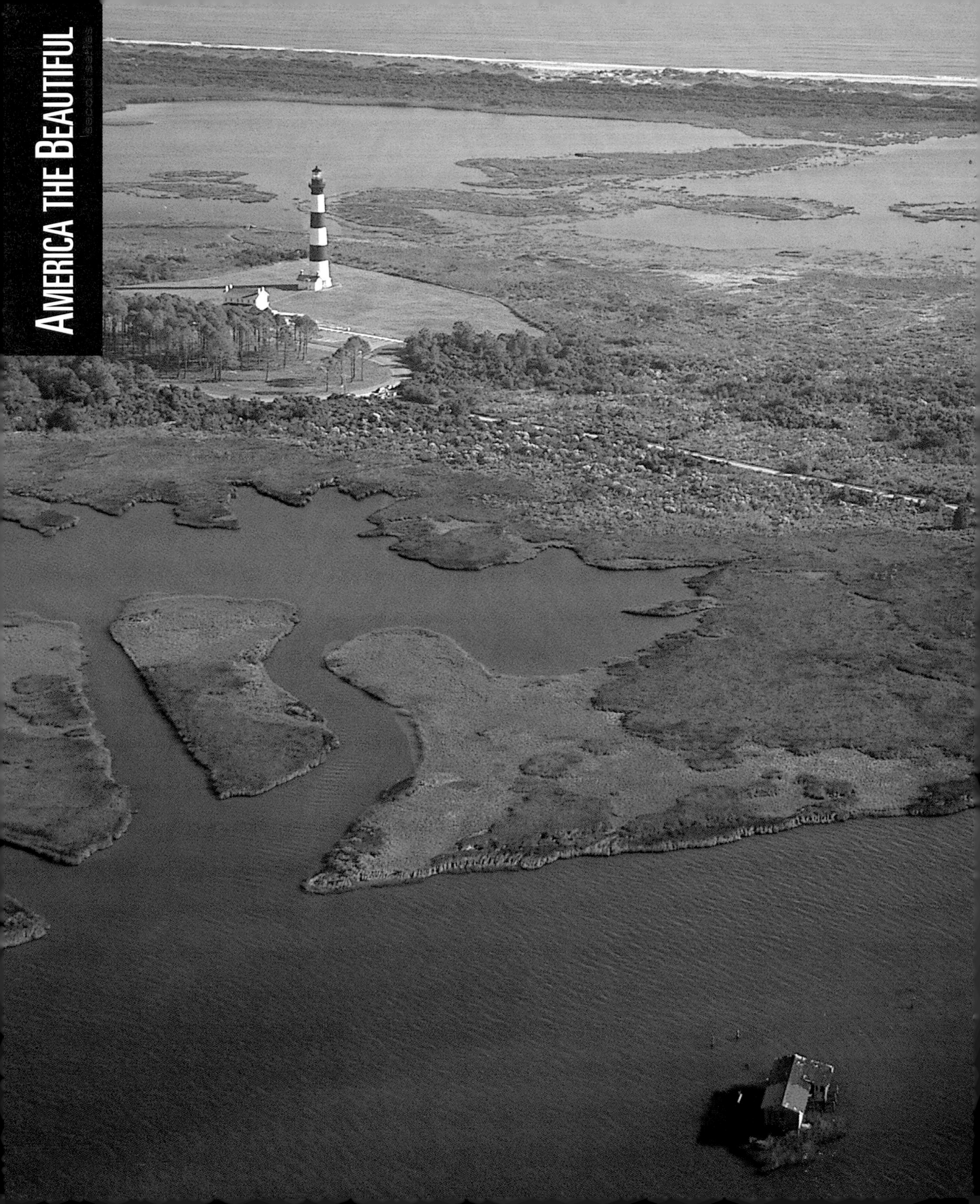
AMERICA THE BEAUTIFUL
second series

North Carolina

Martin Hintz and Stephen Hintz

Children's Press®
A Division of Grolier Publishing
New York   London   Hong Kong   Sydney
Danbury, Connecticut

To the newcomers

Frontispiece: Aerial view of Bodie Island Lighthouse

Front cover: Upper Whitewater Falls, Nantahala National Forest

Back cover: Aerial view of downtown Winston-Salem

Consultant: Ron Jones, Youth Services Consultant, North Carolina State Archives

Please note: All statistics are as up-to-date as possible at the time of publication.

Visit Children's Press on the Internet at http://publishing.grolier.com

Book production by Editorial Directions, Inc.

Library of Congress Cataloging-in-Publication Data

Hintz, Martin.
    North Carolina / by Martin Hintz and Stephen Hintz.
      p. cm. — (America the beautiful. Second series)
    Includes bibliographical references (p.) and index.
    Summary : An introduction to the geography, history, natural resources, economy,
people, and interesting sites of North Carolina.
   ISBN 0-516-20638-9
   1. North Carolina—Juvenile literature. [1. North Carolina.] I. Hintz, Stephen V.
II. Title. III. Series.
F254.3.H56 1998
975.6—dc21   97-44305
                                                      CIP
                                                        AC

Acknowledgments

The authors extend their thanks for help in research, suggestions, and ideas to the North Carolina Department of Commerce and the School Information Program of the Travel and Tourism Division; the Industrial Development Division of the Department of Commerce; the State Library of North Carolina Web Team; and the North Carolina History Museum. We especially want to thank the many North Carolinian people who were eloquent in telling the story of their state. They were just being themselves.

State capitol

Lake Mattamuskeet

Young North Carolinians

Bodie Island
Lighthouse

Contents

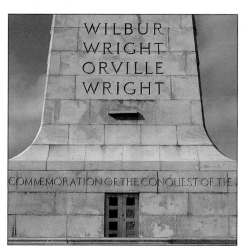

The Wright Memorial

Fishing at Cape Hatteras

Grandfather Mountain

Cardinal

CHAPTER ONE

Hello, North Carolina

The front porch of
Balsam Mountain Inn

North Carolina is a region of rugged mountains and cypress swamps, soaring buildings and raging waters, peaceful villages and bustling cities. It is a state that is steeped in history, yet vigorous today and eager to face tomorrow's challenges.

The state can be as simple and comfortable as a well-worn slipper. The people of North Carolina enjoy sitting on the front porch, sipping lemonade, and nodding to passersby. The town of Black Mountain, deep in the Swannanoa Valley, actually calls itself the "front porch of western North Carolina." It earned the nickname because so many of its tidy brick homes have a well-used porch where homeowners can watch the world go by. Sometimes, porch-sitting is part of business in North Carolina. In the 1850s, wealthy shopkeeper John Moore insisted that the proposed new Main Street in his hometown of Mooresville curve away from the railroad tracks. He wanted to see if farm wagons stopped at his store near the depot while he sat on his front steps after lunch.

Opposite: The Blue
Ridge Parkway

Geopolitical map of North Carolina

This is a state where friendliness is taken for granted. Courtesy too is part of North Carolina, where most young people say "Yes sir" and "Yes ma'am" to adults.

Added Adventure

Sure, you can sit on a porch in this state. But adventure is everywhere too. In Pisgah National Forest, you can slip and slide down a 60-foot (18-m) waterfall into a refreshing pool. Or you can totter across the mile-high swinging bridge that connects two peaks of Grandfather Mountain. Try the take-your-breath-away windsurfing and parasailing on the Outer Banks. Or cast for trout in the cold streams of the Nantahala National Forest.

Try cycling along the twisting Connemara Trail in the Blue Ridge Mountains. The road's fast return run will put your heart in

Hang-gliding instruction

your mouth when you swoop back down the 2,400-foot (732-m) slope.

Even the state's business world has a fast-paced edge beneath its "good ol' boy" facade. Corporate headquarters and financial institutions tower above the streets of Charlotte, Winston-Salem, and Raleigh, where North Carolinians make multimillion-dollar deals. The cities themselves seem to be in an upward rush of glass and steel.

The financial district in Charlotte

Athletic Competition

Competition is just as intense on the athletic field. The nation's top pros and amateurs battle on the basketball court, the soccer field, and the football gridiron. College and high-school games and tournaments get headlines in North Carolina. On an individual level, athletes compete in marathon running, long-distance cycling, and swimming.

For a change of pace, you can watch the thundering race cars at the state's many raceways. They seem to symbolize North Carolina's rush into the future.

The Arts and the Artists

North Carolina's artists dazzle the eye with brilliant canvases and monumental sculptures. Museums and galleries host shows by internationally acclaimed painters. On the music scene, rock-and-roll concerts are attended by thousands. And then, on a quiet drive along a mountain road, you may hear the strains of a fiddle played just for the sheer fun of it.

Ballet and folk dancers swirl and twirl across a dozen stages, and symphonies and folk musicians cast their magic spells. North Carolina's actors and actresses perform the works of the world's best playwrights, and plays are staged in hundreds of venues, from school auditoriums to modern repertory theaters.

The North Carolina Dance Theater

Sports enthusiasts enjoy cross-country skiing in winter.

State for All Seasons

North Carolina is certainly a state for all seasons. It is typical of states in the South, with its warm breezes and dogwood blossoms. But you can also capture the thrill of downhill skiing at Sugar Mountain or follow quiet cross-country trails at Moses H. Cone Park.

At the Appalachian Cultural Museum in Boone, you can learn how early settlers lived. You can visit Kings Mountain National Military Park, where, at the start of the American Revolution, rebellious mountain men defeated their Loyalist neighbors. Visit South Building on the campus of the University of North Carolina–Chapel Hill where U.S. president James Polk, class of 1818, once lived. Along the Blue Ridge Parkway, look for the Linville Caverns where soldiers hid out in the Civil War.

Of course, the state has its share of problems. There is poverty amid the prosperity—run-down shacks as well as luxurious mansions. Homeless citizens rub elbows with corporate executives on downtown streets. Today's challenges also include ensuring clean water and air, protecting the environment, maintaining good schools, and providing health care. Family services, too, always need strengthening. But North Carolinians generally take such problems in stride and work to overcome them.

It is easy to get into the flow of life in North Carolina. Just

pick up a gee-haw whimmy diddle—a stick with notches carved along the top and a propeller loosely nailed to one end. Rub the notches with another stick and the propeller turns. This is a folk toy from the old days, and children yelled "gee" when rubbing on the right side of the stick and "haw" when rubbing on the left. Everyone tried to do the same move and yell at the same time as their friends, like farmers yelling "gee" and "haw" to direct their mules as they plowed the fields. If you listen closely, the words even sound like a mule braying.

Nowadays, nobody needs to yell "gee" and "haw" at mules. Tractors are more common on modern North Carolina farms than mules are. But sometimes yelling just does you good.

Kayaking is a favorite sport on North Carolina's rivers.

CHAPTER TWO

North Carolina's Beginnings

The written history of North Carolina goes back 400 years to the days when Europeans settled here. But people have lived in this area for more than 10,000 years. As the glaciers retreated at the end of the last Ice Age, the first nomadic hunters entered the region in pursuit of wild game. No doubt they found plenty to eat in the mountains and plains of what is now North Carolina.

Over the centuries, the ancestors of today's Native American nations made their way into North Carolina and established tribal territories. Along the coast were the Chowan, Machapunga, Moratok, Pamlico, Secoton, Weapomeoc, Hatteras, and Yammassee. Just inland were the Meherrin and Corree. Building villages and setting up farms in the Piedmont were the Catawba, Waxhaw, Tuscarora, and Chowanoc tribes. The Cherokee lived in the hill country and readily adapted to the mountainous terrain. Each group had its own customs, dress, and language.

Town Creek Indian Mound

Five miles (8 km) southeast of Mount Gilead in the Charlotte area is the Town Creek Indian Mound State Historic Site. In the sixteenth century, this area was a cultural and religious center for a group of American Indians related to the Creek. The tribe farmed the rich soil along the Little River. The palisade wall that enclosed the grounds has been reconstructed. A rebuilt temple atop a man-made mound of earth looks out over the landscape. The visitor center offers a film and slide show depicting the lives and work of these Native Americans. ■

The Cherokee

Eventually, the Cherokee became the most prominent Indian tribe in Carolina. Physically, they were taller and stronger than their neighbors—attributes that gave them an advantage. The Cherokee

Opposite: Cherokee in traditional dress

A young woman attends the annual dance festival at Town Creek Indian Mound.

were also excellent hunters who went far from their homes looking for deer, bear, wild turkey, and other game. Gooseberries, mushrooms, herbs, and hickory nuts were plentiful. Fields were planted with maize (or corn), beans, squash, pumpkins, and tobacco.

Unlike the wandering Plains Indians of America's Far West who lived in easily transported tepees—shelters made of buffalo hide—Carolina's American Indians built settled communities. At first, their huts were simply made of split cane, brush, and twigs, covered with bark roofs. In later years, these flimsy structures were replaced with log hogans—wooden houses covered with hardened clay. During very cold weather, families curled up in their hothouses, small structures near the main buildings. These were built partly underground and covered with dirt or clay to keep in the heat.

American Indian villages, sometimes consisting of 100 or more families, were usually located near the mouth of a river or along a stream where there was fresh water to drink and plenty of fish to eat. The Cherokee developed the most advanced political system of all of Carolina's Native Americans. They had seven clans, with such names as Wild Potato and Long Hair, and an elected council of nine men and seven women who looked after the affairs of all the Cherokee. Women were highly respected. They were also warriors and could vote for their council leaders.

Europeans Arrive

When the Europeans arrived in the sixteenth century, there were probably about 35,000 Native Americans living in North Carolina,

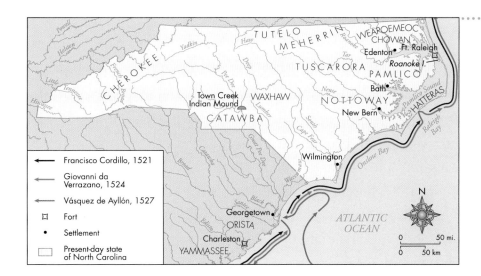

Exploration of North Carolina

but the arrival of the whites had a devastating effect. Disease, war, and forced emigration resulted in fewer than 2,000 American Indians living in the region 300 years later.

The Spanish were the first outsiders to explore the Carolina coast. Francisco Cordillo's men sailed along the Carolina shoreline in 1521. Then Giovanni da Verrazano, an Italian navigator in the service of France, explored the area between Cape Fear and Kitty Hawk during the summer of 1524. A report of his discoveries was published in a journal called *Voyages Touching the Discoverie of America.* In 1527, Lucas Vásquez de Ayllón established a colony where Georgetown, South Carolina, stands today, but disease and starvation forced the settlers to move south.

No other Europeans arrived until 1585, when English explorer Sir Walter Raleigh sent two ships to Carolina. He was commissioned by Queen Elizabeth I to establish a settlement to secure England's territorial claims. Raleigh and others founded the first English colony in North America on Roanoke Island, and Fort Raleigh was built. The colony of "Virginia," which included what

Painting of Sir Walter Raleigh on board his ship

are now North Carolina and South Carolina, was named for Elizabeth I, known as the "Virgin Queen." When they arrived on the frontier, Raleigh's captains found a land with plentiful wildlife and lush vegetation. The American Indians they met gave them freshly caught fish in exchange for clothing.

In 1587, another group of 100 men and women arrived from England and built a second colony. It was here that Virginia Dare was born, the first child of English-speaking parents in America. This colony is known as the Lost Colony because nobody knows what happened to Virginia Dare or the other colonizers. When another group of settlers arrived several years later, all traces of the village were gone.

A Fort Built

The first permanent white settlers came from the coastal area of Virginia, directly north of North Carolina. In the 1650s, the English constructed a fort at Albermarle Point. Ten years later, they moved to where Charleston, South Carolina, is today. The colonial city quickly became a trading and cultural center, as French, English, and Irish immigrants came to the area to get rich. As the region became more settled, it became known as the Southern Plantation. The governor of Virginia established a "commander" of the Southern Plantation to oversee the area. This office was not filled for long and the position was eventually dropped. Changes in England's affairs set the political climate in North Carolina for the next few years.

The Stuarts became the rulers of England and Scotland after the death of Queen Elizabeth I in 1603. But the Stuart king Charles I was beheaded in a 1649 revolution, and military statesman Oliver Cromwell took power. After Cromwell's death in 1658, another Stuart, Charles II, who had been in exile for nine years, took the throne in 1660. Charles II rewarded his supporters by giving them land in the Virginia colony. Eight of these loyalists, called "proprietors," had the authority to expand business, fishing, mining, and trade from southern Virginia to the Spanish territory of Florida. Carolina lay within this region. The western boundaries of Carolina were never established, however.

A Hard Life

The early Carolinians did not have an easy life. The proprietors had a hard time managing the faraway colony from England. Families

An engraving of Blackbeard, the notorious pirate

had to hack out farms from the wilderness and survive the rugged winters. They also had to deal with the American Indian tribes who resented the white invasion of their lands and fought back as best they could. The Native Americans were gradually pushed aside—with great loss of life on both sides.

During the tumultuous early years of North Carolina, terror often struck from the sea. Pirates ravaged the coastline and hid deep in the coastal swamps. They were led by colorful characters such as Edward Teach, better known as Blackbeard. He was a huge man who often tied glowing embers in his long black beard to scare his opponents. But the fiery Blackbeard eventually met his match in Robert Maynard, a young English navy lieutenant. Maynard met Blackbeard and his flaming beard in 1718 in a fierce shipboard battle at Cape Fear, North Carolina. The officer brought Blackbeard's severed head back to port with him to prove that the fearsome pirate was really dead. Other pirates, such as the brutal Stede Bonnet, who used North Carolina's Outer Banks as a natural hideaway, were also eventually captured and hanged.

Border Disputes

Border disputes with Virginia also disturbed the colonists. To resolve some of these difficulties, the English king took control of all the colonies in North America. In 1729, seven of the eight original proprietors sold their Carolina property back to the king. The lone holdout was John Carteret, earl of Granville, who kept his land until the American Revolution. Royal governors were appointed to run local affairs and generally did a good job managing the colony's affairs. The population increased from 36,000 people in 1729 to about 350,000 in 1775 as Germans, Swiss, Scots-Irish from Northern Ireland, and Highland Scots flooded into the region. They hoped for jobs, the chance to own land, and freedom from the oppression they suffered in their native lands.

Under royal rule, dissatisfaction grew, however. Like the other colonies, North Carolina objected to paying taxes to support England's European wars. Opponents of the king, called the Regulators, protested many colonial policies. The Regulators said they did not have enough input into local government affairs. What started out as fiery speeches escalated into pitched gun battles. The Regulators

A painting of John Carteret, earl of Granville

were finally defeated by Loyalist militia at the Battle of Alamance Creek in 1771.

But the turmoil continued. A group of women known as the Edenton Tea Party signed a document objecting to the king's government. In 1775, the residents of Mecklenburg County supported a breakaway government in western North Carolina. Governor Josiah Martin was literally chased out of the colony by angry North Carolinians in May 1775. He was the last royal governor.

Historical map of
North Carolina

Independence Supported

During the Revolutionary War (1775–1783), most North Carolina residents supported independence from Britain. Those who wanted independence were called Whigs. The supporters of the Crown were Tories. Whig soldiers defeated the Tories at the Battle of

Journey to Statehood

May 20, 1775	A declaration of independence is adopted in Mecklenburg County.
April 12, 1776	North Carolina delegates to the Continental Congress vote for independence.
July 4, 1776	North Carolina delegates sign the Declaration of Independence.
December 1776	The state drafts its first constitution. Richard Caswell becomes the first governor.
November 21, 1789	North Carolina adopts the U.S. Constitution, becoming the twelfth state to join the Union.

Two Capitals and Three Capitols

North Carolina has had two state capitals—New Bern and Raleigh—and three capitols. Tyron Palace in New Bern was built between 1767 and 1770, but the main building was destroyed by fire in 1798. The first capitol in Raleigh was finished in 1794, but it too was destroyed in an 1831 blaze.

The current capitol (left), completed in 1840, is topped with a copper rotunda that glows in the sun. At first, the building was called a "Grecian temple in a hog pasture" because farmers' pigs ran loose in the surrounding area. But the residents soon penned up the hogs, cleaned up the lawn, and built other government buildings in the neighborhood. Raleigh finally looked like a state capital. ■

Moore's Creek Bridge in February 1776—the first battle of the Revolutionary War in North Carolina. On April 12, 1776, North Carolina became the first colony to tell its delegates to the Constitutional Congress to vote for independence. On July 4, the final draft of the Declaration of Independence was signed. Among the signers were North Carolinians Joseph Hewes, John Penn, and William Hooper. In December of that year, Richard Caswell became the first governor of North Carolina.

Constitution Adopted

North Carolina's actions leading up to the Revolutionary War and its statehood demonstrated its citizens' love of freedom and responsibility. North Carolina ratified the U.S. Constitution in 1789, becoming the twelfth former colony to enter the Union. North Carolinians had delayed supporting the Constitution until the Bill of Rights was added. These ten amendments guaranteed freedom

Cherokee, North Carolina

The largest American Indian reservation east of Wisconsin is found in Cherokee, on the western edge of North Carolina. The site was once a hideout for Cherokee who refused to leave the mountains during the Native American removals between the 1820s and 1840s. At that time, the state's tribes were forcibly sent to reservations in the West in a movement called the Trail of Tears. Thousands of people died on the journey.

Visitors can tour the Oconaluftee Indian Village on the reservation, to learn what Cherokee life was like 250 years ago. Today, the Cherokee operate two casinos in town—open twenty-four hours a day for busloads of visiting gamblers. ▪

of speech and other rights for the people, which in those days, however, usually meant only landowners. In fact, only landowners could vote for senators until 1857.

Most African-Americans were slaves who had no rights at all, and free blacks were excluded from voting. Also, many indentured servants from Europe had to work for seven years in near-slavery to pay off their passage to America and did not enjoy as many rights as landowners. But the groundwork being laid would eventually protect the rights of all North Carolinians.

CHAPTER THREE

North Carolina's Teenage Years

North Carolina was a late bloomer when it came to development. In its early years, the state relied heavily on agricultural production and its landowners favored a plantation system that used slave labor. Plantations were huge estates consisting of thousands of acres. It took a large workforce to support such a system, so more and more slaves were brought from Africa. Before the Civil War, slaves made up about one-third of the state's population.

Slaves plant sweet potatoes on James Hopkinson's plantation on Edisto Island.

Families Broken Up

By 1860, North Carolina had more than 300,000 slaves. The colonists' fear of a slave rebellion meant that the Africans had no rights. They were considered valuable property and were bought and sold at the whim of their owners.

Families were broken up when men, women, and children were separated and sent to different plantations. Today, several historic sites in the state show what slave quarters were like.

Constitutional Amendment

In 1835, North Carolina amended its constitution to give more representation to residents in the western part of the state. The amendments fixed the number of state senators at fifty and representatives

Opposite: A cotton field just before harvest

The First Gold Rush

The first documented discovery of gold in the United States occurred in 1799 near Charlotte. One Sunday morning, the son of John Reed, a German immigrant farmer, found a large yellow rock in Little Meadow Creek on Reed's farm. The family thought it made a nice doorstop, not realizing its value. Three years later, a local jeweler offered to buy the rock for $3.50. Reed agreed to the price, unaware that the 17-pound (8-kg) stone in his kitchen was solid gold and worth about one thousand times what the jeweler offered. He finally found out the real value, but a deal was a deal, so Reed went through with it.

However, Reed and his family immediately gave up farming and began searching for gold all over their land. By 1803, Reed had formed a partnership with three other men who mined the region's streams. They found a 28-pound (13-kg) nugget, launching America's first gold rush. It wasn't long before big investors came in and began large-scale underground mining throughout the Piedmont area.

In 1837, the first branch of the United States mint opened in Charlotte, making $5, $2.50, and $1 gold coins. The mint operated until 1913, turning out more than $5 million in coins before it was closed. The building was saved from demolition by local preservationists, and, in 1936, it became the state's first art museum.

The gold found in North Carolina was valued at more than $1 million a year. Then, in 1848, the California gold rush hit. Almost all the miners stampeded West, hoping to make a fortune for themselves rather than having to work for some-

one else. After the Civil War, mining in North Carolina ceased. The Reed Gold Mine is now a state historic site, with a visitor center that shows old mining techniques and highlights a section of the mine. Guests can try their luck at panning for gold in Little Meadow Creek. They may find little nuggets in the stream. North Carolina's gold miners are memorialized by an imposing sculpture in downtown Charlotte (above). ■

at 120. One seat was given to each county and the remainder to counties with the largest populations. However, from 1836 to 1868, the number of senators from an area depended on the amount of taxes that were paid there. This meant that wealthy people had a greater representation than others. The constitution also prevented free blacks from voting, but there was nothing the African-American population could do about that. Nobody paid attention to their requests.

Under the updated constitution, the governor was elected for two years, instead of one year. Edward Bishop Daley was the first governor elected by all the state's eligible voters.

Civil War

As Civil War loomed, North Carolinians were split over issues of states' rights—a principle that emphasized the power of individual states, rather than that of the federal government. Although most North Carolina residents did not own slaves, the idea of slavery was not really questioned. Slavery was so familiar in their world that most white people did not object to it. In May 1861, North Carolina became the last Southern state to secede, or break away from, the Union.

Civil War soldiers proudly sent home photographs of themselves to record their participation in the war.

Many state residents were reluctant to enter the war, but once they did, they fought fiercely. More than 125,000 men joined the Confederate army, which amounted to about 25 percent of the total number of Southern troops. By the end of this dreadful conflict, North Carolina had lost more soldiers to battlefield deaths, wounds, and sickness than any other Confederate state. The state's soldiers boasted that "they were first at Bethel, farthest at Gettys-

North Carolinians in the White House

Three North Carolina natives became presidents of the United States. Andrew Jackson, nicknamed Old Hickory, was the country's seventh president, serving two terms (1828–1836). He was a lawyer, judge, United States senator, and general who defeated the British at the Battle of New Orleans in the War of 1812. Jackson was born on March 15, 1767, in Waxhaw on the border of North and South Carolina.

James K. Polk, the eleventh president of the United States, served from 1844 to 1848. He was born on a farm in Mecklenburg County on November 2, 1795, and moved to Tennessee as a young lawyer. Polk served in both the Tennessee state legislature and in the U.S. Congress. He was a strong advocate of Manifest Destiny— the idea that the United States should spread across North America from the Atlantic to the Pacific Oceans. As president, he almost went to war with England over control of the Oregon Territory. Polk also led the country during the Mexican War (1846–1848), which was fought over the independence of Texas.

Andrew Johnson was born in Raleigh on December 29, 1808. A tailor's apprentice who never formally attended school, he taught himself to read and write with the help of his wife, Eliza. He was active in politics after moving to Tennessee and became a member of the U.S. Congress in 1843. During the Civil War, Johnson was named military governor of Tennessee. He was chosen to be Abraham Lincoln's vice president and became president in 1865 after Lincoln's assassination. He served as the seventeenth president until 1869. Johnson was almost impeached, or removed from office, because Republican senators thought he was too lenient with the defeated South after the war. The impeachment process lost by a single vote. ■

burg, and last at Appomattox." They were referring to the frightful battles that culminated in the surrender of the South's armies. Under the command of General Joseph E. Johnston, the last ragtag North Carolina troops surrendered to Union soldiers led by General William T. Sherman.

A Leader in War and Peace

Zebulon Baird Vance, governor of North Carolina from 1862 to 1865, was typical of many state leaders at the time of the Civil War. His distinguished family had a long record of public service dating from colonial times. His grandfather served with George Washington during the terrible winter encampment at Valley Forge. His father was a captain in the Army during the War of 1812. Other family members were in Congress or held state offices. In 1858, when he was only twenty-eight, Vance followed in their footsteps and was elected to the U.S. House of Representatives, the youngest member of Congress at the time.

Although he was a strong supporter of the Union, Vance felt it more important to support his home state during the war. He became a colonel in the Confederate army, using the built-in support of his dedicated soldiers to win the governor's seat in 1862.

Vance worked hard on behalf of the state's citizens

The Zebulon Vance homestead in Asheville

This famous Thomas Nast cartoon about "carpetbaggers" was published in *Harper's Weekly* in 1877.

during the war. Profits made by selling cotton were used to help North Carolinians. Vance was arrested by Union soldiers when the South surrendered. After the war, he started a law practice in Charlotte, eventually winning the governor's chair again. During this term, occupying federal troops finally left North Carolina. Vance served in the U.S. Senate from 1879 until his death in 1894.

Ruin and Reconstruction

Despite the efforts of such leaders as Vance, North Carolina was devastated for years after the Civil War. Its towns and villages lay in ruins, its plantation system was destroyed, and its government was in disarray. Reconstruction was a frenzied period of hunger and social disorder. Returning soldiers could not find work and feared losing what little they had left. No one knew what to do next. Taking advantage of the situation, carpetbaggers flocked to North Carolina. These were Northerners who saw a chance to make money in the defeated and demoralized South. The Republican-dominated U.S. Congress wanted to punish the South and allowed many abuses by the carpetbaggers to go unchecked.

The newly freed blacks were often used for unscrupulous purposes. Former slaves who could not read or write were put into businesses and political office without proper training and support. Behind the scenes, outsiders pulled the strings and stole money for themselves. In a backlash, white supremacist groups like the Ku Klux Klan sprang up to frighten the blacks back into submission. Klan members wore white sheets to hide their identities and thundered through the countryside, lynching African-Americans and terrorizing anyone who disagreed with them. Their legacy of hate has still not died out.

However, most North Carolinians were law-abiding citizens who wanted to put the horror of war behind them and worked hard to put their state on a good economic footing. The state was admitted back into the Union in 1868 after adopting a new constitution. Testifying to the foresight of its writers, thirty of that constitution's amendments are still in force.

The Ku Klux Klan burned crosses to frighten African-Americans into submission.

Sharecropper System

After the war, the planters divided up their land and rented it to poor whites and blacks. They charged high rents and exorbitant prices for seed and food at the local stores, which, generally, they also owned. The farmers had to share part of their crops with the landowners to pay the bills they owed. This was the start of the "sharecropping" system, which put the farmers at a great disadvantage. Because they had little investment money of their own, there was nothing on which they could fall back. It was hard to get out from under the financial burden.

New Beginnings

Yet within thirty years after the war, North Carolinians had slowly put order back into their lives. On the cultural front, the state

Public Schools

North Carolina's first school was set up at Symons Creek near Elizabeth City in 1705, but initial attempts to establish public schools were opposed by religious groups who said churches should be in charge of all education. However, the state's 1776 constitution established a public school system and chartered the University of North Carolina, which began offering classes in 1795. It was the first state university in the nation. ■

passed its first law providing aid to public libraries in 1887, and the first tax-supported library opened its doors in Durham.

North Carolina remained primarily an agricultural state, basing its economy on its abundant natural resources. Cotton and tobacco were the state's main cash crops. North Carolina's thick forests provided wood for the state's growing furniture industry, pumping millions of dollars into the economy.

The Three R's

In 1901, Governor Charles B. Aycock supported a strong public school system throughout the state, marking a turning point in North Carolina history. He advocated higher pay and better training for teachers and more classrooms. These improvements laid the groundwork for the state's generally excellent educational system today.

The Vanderbilts

In 1895, the 250-room Biltmore Estate in Asheville was constructed as a home for twenty-six-year-old multimillionaire George W. Vanderbilt. Vanderbilt, grandson of tycoon Cornelius Vanderbilt, built his home in Asheville because he liked the mountain views and pleasant climate. He purchased 125,000 acres (50,586 ha) of land and made his house the centerpiece. The entrance road to the home was 3 miles (4.8 km) long.

The construction of the building took 1,000 workers five years. The workers were housed in a specially built village near the site, and a private railroad line was run onto the property for transporting construction materials. Lovely formal gardens surrounded the house. Vanderbilt also wanted his grounds to be a working farm so that the place would pay for itself. He was a Vanderbilt—a shrewd businessman who demanded that everything carry its own weight.

Today the estate is among North Carolina's most popular tourist sites, visited by tens of thousands of visitors each year. When the house was opened to the public in 1930, people were amazed to find it had indoor plumbing, a refrigerator, electric lights, and central heating. The walls of the breakfast room were covered in Spanish leather.

Only 8,000 acres (3,000 ha) of the original estate are still owned by the Vanderbilt family. The remainder have become part of the Blue Ridge Parkway and nearby Pisgah National Forest. ■

CHAPTER FOUR

North Carolina Grows Up

In the early 1900s, textile mills became the state's major employers, and many farmers left their overworked land to find jobs in the fast-growing cities. Even children worked in the factories. However, some of the more established city residents looked down on these hungry, eager-to-work newcomers. When they lived on the farms, they were nicknamed "rednecks" because of the red clay dust that caked their necks after working in the fields. When they began to labor long hours in the factories, they were called "lint-heads." Both terms were fighting words for a long time.

Children working at a cotton mill

For corporate executives, however, everything was going well. The influx of cheap labor held down costs and kept profits up, and the demand for North Carolina's textiles and other products was rising worldwide. More than 86,000 men joined the armed services during World War I (1914–1918), and some 800 lost their lives. Veterans returned to pick up where they had left off. Generally, the sad legacy of the Civil War was left far behind, except for the troubled relationships between the races—a problem that continued well into the twentieth century.

Opposite: Manufacturing polyester fabric at Burlington Industries' weaving plant in Cordova

Better and Worse

Prosperity meant that many civic improvements could be undertaken. Government buildings, bridges, dams, and other buildings were constructed. By the 1920s, the state had such a far-reaching highway-building program that North Carolina was often called the Good Road State.

But then trouble struck with terrible swiftness, affecting every North Carolinian—the wealthy, the middle class, and the poor. The Great Depression of the 1930s was a worldwide economic collapse in which banks closed and tens of thousands of people lost their jobs and their homes, their farms, and their businesses. Fortunes disappeared overnight. People struggled to survive and keep their families together. Many North Carolinians headed north toward what they hoped were better opportunities. Often they were dis-

Many banks, like the Raleigh Banking & Trust Company, closed their doors during the Great Depression.

appointed. State and federal governments were at a loss—they had no social safety nets in place at that time. It was up to friends and family to help one another as much as they could through the hard days.

Roosevelt Elected

Democratic President Franklin D. Roosevelt accepted the country's challenge when he was elected in 1932. He promised a "New Deal" to give the people the relief they needed. The federal government stepped in to guarantee bank deposits, so that no one would lose money if a bank failed. Electricity was brought to rural areas. The unemployed went to work in federal government programs such as the Civilian Conservation Corps (CCC). Eager young men constructed campgrounds, cabins, and

Recruits of the First Forest Army on their way to a reforestation camp in President Roosevelt's CCC program

trails in the state's forests and parks. They did such a good job that their work still stands.

World War II (1939–1945) returned some prosperity to North Carolina because America needed the state's corn, tobacco, cotton, and peanuts. Textiles, furniture, and other products headed to new markets that suddenly opened up. Patriotic North Carolinians responded with 361,388 men and 5,170 women in the armed services.

The realities of war came very close to North Carolina. The sea-lanes off the Outer Banks were called Torpedo Alley because German submarines attacked merchant ships there as they headed off to Europe. People who lived along the coast often saw the flames of burning vessels on the horizon, and wreckage and bodies washed up on shore.

Peace and Plenty

Life in North Carolina returned to normal after the war, but it was faster paced. There was more money to be made in the demand for manufactured goods. And improved farming methods helped increase crop yields, cut down on soil erosion, and resolved other environmental problems. From the 1950s through the 1970s, North Carolina slowly continued its changeover from a primarily rural, agricultural state to an urban, industrialized state.

Sit-ins and Civil Rights

Prosperity and equality, however, were not extended to all North Carolina citizens for many years. From the time they were shipped to North America from Africa as slaves to the middle of the twentieth century, black Americans were excluded from the state's political and economic life. Few African-Americans could vote. Their separate schools were inferior to the schools for white children. Blacks and whites could not even use the same bathrooms or drink from the same water fountains. The sign "Colored Only" was a constant reminder of this inequality. There was a bitter joke that African-Americans were equal only when they were standing up—at a bank window to deposit their savings, at the utility company counter to pay their bills, or at cash registers in stores.

Black children experienced segregation and were forced to accept separate facilities.

But the invisible line of segregation was drawn when they wanted to sit down in a restaurant, theater, or any other public place. They were always supposed to go to the back of the bus, sit in the balcony, or be seen only where their second-class status could be emphasized. It made no difference that African-Americans were often veterans of America's wars or nannies who took care of white children. They were not considered equal to even the poorest whites. These unfortunate segregationist ideas were a deeply ingrained part of the Deep South.

So something had to give. Centuries of frustration and anger spilled over, with an entire race demanding the rights granted to all other citizens. During the civil rights movement of the 1960s, Greensboro, North Carolina, became a landmark. In 1960, four black students refused to leave a whites-only lunch counter in a local restaurant. They staged a sit-in—they wouldn't get out of their seats even when they were threatened with arrest.

This brave act of rebellion and demand for equal service in Greensboro sparked similar demonstrations throughout the South and raised white America's awareness of the black Americans' struggle for dignity. Open-minded whites joined their black neighbors to reverse the consequences of years of racial separation. The national Civil Rights Act of 1964 can trace its success partially to the hard-fought social battles waged by thousands of ordinary North Carolinians of all colors who simply wanted all races to be treated with equal respect.

Intense racial problems broke out again in the mid-1990s, with a rash of church burnings throughout the rural South. African-American congregations were hit most often and North Carolina

Opposite: A sit-in at the F. W. Woolworth store in Greensboro

Maya Angelou

Maya Angelou is many things—poet, historian, author, actress, playwright, civil rights activist, producer, and director. She lectures widely around the world from Wake Forest University in Winston-Salem, North Carolina, where she is a professor of American studies. A noted author, Angelou has published ten best-selling books and written countless magazine articles. She wrote and delivered a poem for President Clinton's 1993 presidential inauguration.

Angelou began her career in drama and dance. She then married a South African civil rights organizer and lived in Cairo, Egypt, where she became editor of *The Arab Observer*—the only English-language news weekly in the Middle East. In Ghana, West Africa, she was feature editor of *The African Review* and taught at the University of Ghana. Back home in the 1960s, Angelou became the northern coordinator for the Southern Christian Leadership Conference, a major civil rights groups. She was then appointed by President Gerald Ford to the Bicentennial Commission and by President Jimmy Carter to the National Commission on the Observance of International Women's Year.

Angelou has broken ground for black women in film and broadcasting, and has made hundreds of TV appearances. Her autobiographical account of her childhood years, *I Know Why the Cage Bird Sings* (1970), was a television special. Angelou has also written and produced several prize-winning documentaries, including *Afro-Americans in the Arts*. The multilingual Angelou is fluent in French, Spanish, Italian, and West African Fanti, as well as English. ◼

was not immune. Mount Moriah Baptist Church in Hillsborough, Mount Tabor Baptist Church in Cerro Gordo, Pleasant Hill Baptist Church in Lumberton, and Matthews-Murkland Presbyterian Church in Charlotte were destroyed by arson in 1995 and 1996.

Investigators sort through the charred remains of the Matthews-Murkland Presbyterian Church.

Investigators are still trying to find the people responsible for these hate crimes.

Efforts and Awards

All North Carolinians are concerned about social problems and are working hard to resolve them. The American Civil Liberties Union (ACLU) chapter in North Carolina gives annual awards to individuals who have a lifelong commitment to protecting and enhancing civil rights. Congresswoman Eva Clayton, the first African-American to be elected to the U.S. Congress from North Carolina since 1901, and former Charlotte mayor Harvey Gantt were among those honored.

Citizen Action of North Carolina has taken another approach. It researches special-interest campaign contributions to elected

Harvey Gantt, former Charlotte mayor, has been recognized by the ACLU for his work on behalf of civil rights.

officials in an effort to stop big-money interests from dictating public policy in North Carolina. The organization wants political leaders held accountable for their decisions on recycling, environmental cleanup, lower utility rates, and similar issues. In addition, the Sierra Club and other environmental organizations actively support the protection of North Carolina's pristine wilderness, as well as its clean water and air and its efforts to slow urban sprawl.

In 1996, Raleigh-Durham ranked fifth among the nation's best places to live and work, according to *Fortune* magazine. "This is one more testament to our efforts to provide good jobs and a top-quality environment for our families," said Governor Jim Hunt, offering his congratulations to the two cities.

Other North Carolina communities continue to grow as glittering business centers. In May 1997, *Inc.* magazine placed Charlotte and the high-tech world of Raleigh-Durham among the best small-business neighborhoods in the nation—great places to begin a new business. The magazine cited North Carolinians' "can-do" attitudes, available start-up money, and quality workforce.

A State in the Spotlight

The world is also looking at North Carolina. In 1997, for example, the American Council on Germany held its Young Leaders Conference in Durham. At this annual conference, which encourages

Congresswoman Eva Clayton meets President Bill Clinton at a meeting of business leaders in Washington, D.C.

cooperation between the United States and Germany, fifty young professionals from business, government, the media, and the education world met to discuss political, social, and economic issues.

In addition to welcoming overseas leaders, North Carolina actively pursues business and cultural links with other countries. Governor Hunt and his predecessors have led trade missions to many nations, including Israel, South Africa, Japan, and Mexico, to promote international trade and corporate relocations. Their efforts have paid off. By 1997, 25 percent of the businesses investing in North Carolina were foreign companies.

In keeping with the state's forward thrust, community leaders in the Greensboro/Winston-Salem/High Point area are working hard to get a Major League Baseball team to settle there by 2000. They expect that this will be another measure of their community success.

CHAPTER FIVE

From the Sea to the Mountains

North Carolina is the twenty-ninth largest state in the United States. It is sandwiched between Virginia on the north, Georgia and South Carolina on the south, and Tennessee on the west. The rolling waters of the Atlantic Ocean wash up on the east coast, with a 301-mile (484-km)-long coastline.

The state encompasses 52,672 square miles (136,420 sq km) of mountains, plains, and seacoast. Its greatest distance from north to south is 188 miles (303 km). The greatest distance from east to west is 499 miles (803 km).

There are 3,954 square miles (10,241 sq km) of inland waters. Lake Mattamuskeet, North Carolina's largest natural lake, is 15 miles (24 km) long and 6 miles (10 km) wide.

Birds frequent the shores of Lake Mattamuskeet.

Three Geographical Sections

All this land and water is divided into three main geographic sections. From west to east are the Mountain Region, the Piedmont,

Opposite: Sunset at Cape Fear, Bald Head Island

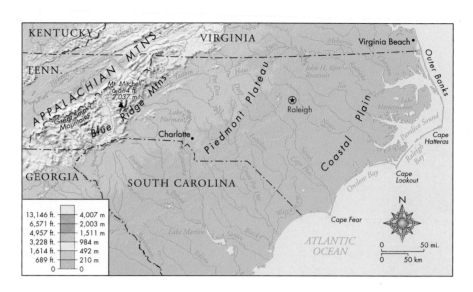

North Carolina's topography

and the Atlantic Coastal Plain. When looking at a map, think of the state as a downhill slope from left to right. The state's highest point is Mount Mitchell at 6,684 feet (2,037 m) in the far west. From this mountainous region, North Carolina slides toward sea level at the ocean.

For an overview of North Carolina's topography, let's start at the bottom—the Coastal Plain. This stretch of beaches, low islands, and sand dunes runs all the way from New Jersey to southern Florida. Sandbars, inlets, river mouths, and islands make up the state's shoreline. The soils here range from peat—partly decayed plant matter usually found in swamps—to sand and sandy loam— a mixture of dirt and sand.

A long line of sandbars called the Outer Banks lie along the coast. They are the remains of an ancient seabed, a reminder of several prehistoric Ice Ages when the ocean level was much lower. The Outer Banks were formed about 20,000 years ago. At that

Bodie Island Light-house on the Outer Banks

time, the land that is now North Carolina extended another 13 miles (21 km) farther into the ocean because the water was some 400 feet (120 m) lower than it is today. As the polar ice caps began to melt, the ocean level rose. Thousands of years passed, and silt from rivers piled up behind the dunes. But as the sea rose, the dunes were submerged and the ocean formed the sounds (bays) behind the then-underwater dunes. Over the centuries, the rising ocean slowed to where it now rises only about 12 inches (30 cm) every 100 years. The tips of the dunes peaked from the surface, plant life took hold, and the Outer Banks came to life.

Today, the Outer Banks are about 12 feet (4 m) above the ocean, ranging from 3,000 feet (914 m) to about 3 miles (5 km) across. Until the 1930s, when bridges were built from the mainland, the Outer Banks were relatively inaccessible except by boat or airplane. To help protect the area, the Cape Hatteras National Seashore was dedicated in 1953.

Outer Banks Protection

The Outer Banks protect the mainland from some of the ocean's erosive effects, and travelers vacation on the unspoiled shores, especially near Cape Hatteras. But the shifting sands are always dangerous. Numerous ships have run aground or sunk because of these treacherous sands. Early sailors called the most dangerous sites Cape Lookout and Cape Fear for good reason.

Coastal Link

North Carolina's coastline includes reedy marshland, cypress swamps, shallow lakes, and meandering rivers. Dismal Swamp, one

of the nation's largest swamps, stretches from the state's far northeast corner up through southeastern Virginia. At first glance, its towering black gum trees, moss-covered cypresses, shaded creeks, and thick underbrush look ominous. But this area is rich in natural resources and is an important watershed. The eastern border of the swamp is an ancient beach called the Nansemond escarpment, or steep slope. The swamp, only 10 to 22 feet (3 to 7 m) above sea level, is from 20 to 30 miles (32 km to 48 km) long and 10 to 20 miles (16 km to 32 km) wide. Lake Drummond is the largest body of water in the swamp, ranging from 6 to 10 feet (2 to 3 m) deep,

Cape Lookout extends far out into the ocean.

WILBUR WRIGHT
ORVILLE WRIGHT

IN COMMEMORATION OF THE CONQUEST OF THE AIR

First Flight

The Wright Memorial (above) on the Outer Banks symbolizes a new era for transportation. Here, Wilbur and Orville Wright flew the first heavier-than-air craft, a flight that lasted only 12 seconds and traveled a mere 120 feet (36.5 m). But this modest beginning set the stage for today's jet airplanes and spaceships.

The Wright brothers came to the North Carolina coast from Ohio. U.S. Weather Bureau records showed that this was where they could find steady winds strong enough to lift their gliders.

Between 1901 and 1902, the Wrights made more than 1,000 glider flights from these sand dunes. On December 17, 1903, they decided to try out their fragile airplane, powered by a small engine. The plane took off from an 80-foot (24-m) starting ramp on Kill Devil Hill, halfway between Kitty Hawk and Nag's Head. The flight was successful, and history was made. ■

depending on the rainfall. The swamp used to be much larger but sections were drained to build a ship canal between Chesapeake Bay and Albemarle Sound. In addition, much of the forestland has been cut down. Environmental activists, greatly concerned about the shrinking size of the swamp, have at last been able to get the state to limit the development there.

The grassy prairie just inland from the coast has few trees. This is savannah country, wide stretches of fertile open ground that provide good pasture for dairy cattle. However, most dairy farming is more inland in the area from Raleigh west to Iredell County. The western rim of the coastal plain has the best agricultural land in North Carolina. To the south, winds and waves have created sandhills that roll to the horizon.

Visitors canoe through the Dismal Swamp.

Piedmont Heartland

The state's heartland is the Piedmont, a succession of rolling hills that make central North Carolina look like a rumpled quilt. The red-clay tobacco-growing region covers 44 of the state's 100 counties. Here, about 300 feet (90 m) above sea level, the landscape begins its rise toward the crown of Mount Mitchell in the west. The imaginary border between the hills and the plain is known as the Fall Line. The Piedmont slowly rises to about 1,500 feet (460 m) above the sea at the edge of the mountains. Most

The red clay of the Piedmont colors the water of Lake Norman.

Appalachian Rocks

Rocks making up the Appalachian chain can be very valuable. In the late 1800s, rare gems such as the pigeon-blood ruby were discovered in North Carolina. Sapphires, kyanite, moonstone, garnets, and other stones can still be found. Almost half of the feldspar mined in the United States comes from near Spruce Pine. The ground-up chalky-textured rock is used in a range of products, from paint to plates. ■

North Carolinians live in the Piedmont, where the state's industry is concentrated.

On the west, rugged mountain ranges and dense forests run from Pennsylvania to Georgia, covering 11,000 square miles (28,500 sq km). The best-known range is the Blue Ridge, North Carolina's major stretch of mountains. Others are the Unaka, Bald, Black, Stone, South, Great Smoky, and Brushy ranges. These are all part of the ancient Appalachian Mountains, which are older than the Swiss Alps and the Himalaya in Asia. Millions of years of erosion have worn these once-giant ranges down to their present height. Mount Mitchell, the highest peak east of the

Mississippi River, is one of forty granite mountains more than 6,000 feet (1,820 m) high. Deep gorges and rocky outcroppings scar the faces of the mountains, creating interesting images. Chimney Rock is a towering stone pedestal, more than 250 feet (76 m) high, while Grandfather Mountain looks like an old man lying on his back.

Grandfather Mountain

The Blue Ridge Parkway

The Blue Ridge Parkway was built in 1935, partly to provide employment during the Great Depression. The road links Shenandoah National Park in Virginia and the Great Smoky Mountains National Park on the North Carolina–Tennessee border. About 200 miles (320 km) of the parkway's total 470 miles (756 km) are within the state of North Carolina itself. Landscape architect Stanley Abbott wanted the highway to connect travelers to the land and inspire future generations to preserve the surrounding wilderness.

Work is continuing to improve the roadway, with the completion of Linn Cove Viaduct at Grandfather Mountain. The 1,243-foot (379-m) S-shaped bridge, completed in 1983, has a span that swings out high as it swoops around several bends before rejoining the side of the mountain.

Many overlooks add interest along the way. The Pisgah National Forest is named after the biblical mountain where Moses saw the Promised Land. Historical homes, craft centers, out-of-the way restaurants, and remains of pioneer cabins dot the route. Outdoor lovers will find picnic tables and plenty of horseback riding, hiking, and campgrounds. Friends of the Blue Ridge Parkway, a volunteer group, sponsors Grover Groundhog's Nature Club for Kids. The club helps young people learn about the Blue Ridge Mountains and the importance of protecting them. Dead trees along the towering slopes of Mount Mitchell point out the result of acid rain and the need for environmental vigilance. ■

Rivers Rise

Most of North Carolina's rivers rise in the mountains and flow toward the sea. Many lovely waterfalls tumble over the Fall Line. Whitewater Falls is a photographer's delight. The 411-foot (125-m) drop near Cashiers, a small town in western North Carolina, is one of the largest and loveliest waterfalls in the eastern United States. At the coastal plain, the rivers broaden as they flow downstream from the hills. The state's major rivers are the Roanoke, Neuse, Tar, Pamlico, and Cape Fear. Where streams and rivers drain westward from the Blue Ridge Mountains into Tennessee, several large dams provide electrical power. These waterways include the Nantahala, Little Tennessee, and the Hiwassee.

Vegetation has adapted to North Carolina's many land features. Pine woods stretch along the coastal plains. Some bizarre species have evolved too. The Croatan National Forest has at least eleven insect-eating plants, including Venus's-flytrap and butter-

Whitewater Falls in Nantahala National Forest

North Carolina's Geographical Features

Total area; rank	52,672 sq. mi. (136,420 sq km); 29th
Land; rank	48,718 sq. mi. (126,179 sq km); 29th
Water; rank	3,954 sq. mi. (10,241 sq km); 10th
Inland water; rank	3,954 sq. mi. (10,241 sq km); 6th
Geographic center	Chatham, 10 mi. (16 km) northwest of Sanford
Highest point	Mount Mitchell, 6,684 feet (2,037 m)
Lowest point	Sea level along the Atlantic coast
Largest city	Charlotte
Longest river	Cape Fear River, 200 miles (320 km)
Population; rank	6,657,630 (1990 census); 10th
Record high temperature	109°F (43°C) at Albemarle on July 28, 1940
Record low temperature	−29°F (−34°C) at Mount Mitchell on January 30, 1966
Average July temperature	70°F (21°C)
Average January temperature	41°F (5°C)
Average annual precipitation	50 inches (127 cm)

The kudzu vines creep over everything.

wort. In the low country, oaks are draped in Spanish moss, with jasmine and honeysuckle growing wild along the ditches. In summer, the green of kudzu is everywhere, its long vines smothering telephone poles and fences. The kudzu was brought to the South in the 1870s from Asia in the hope that the vines would stop riverbank erosion. But the plant takes over everything and is now called the Scourge of the South.

Flora, Fauna, and Climate

While ragged stands of oak and pine groves dot the Piedmont, the mountain forests are thick. Sycamores, sourwoods, hemlock, oak, red spruce, hickory, and other trees are abundant in the hill country. In spring, colorful wildflowers bloom across the ridges and in the valleys. Lady's slippers, trilliums, and jack-in-the-pulpits paint a brilliant scene.

North Carolina is home to many wild animals. The black bears

North Carolina's parks and forests

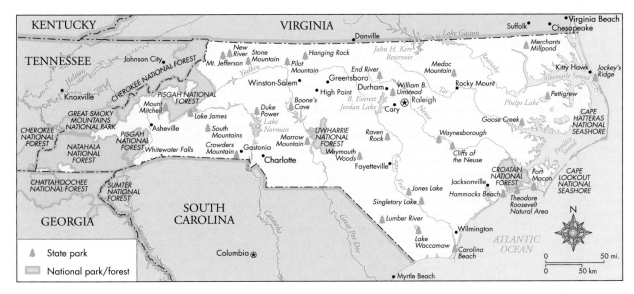

here are big—up to 300 pounds (136 kg). More than 400 bears live in Great Smoky Mountains National Park where they forage for berries and hunt small animals. Other state animals include beaver, white-tailed deer, mink, fox, bobcats, wild turkeys, woodchucks, and hundreds of bird, fish, and reptile species.

North Carolina's weather is as varied as its wildlife. Generally, the temperature range is quite pleasant. In the coastal plain, the annual mean temperature is 61.1°F (16°C), with an average of 46.5°F (8°C) in January and 79.1°F (26°C) in July. In the Piedmont area, the average mean temperature is 60.2°F (15°C), with an average of 41.2°F (5°C) in January and 78.4°F (25.5°C) in July. In the mountains, the average mean temperature is 54.1°F (12°C), with 35.4°F (2°C) in January and 71.7°F (22°C) in July. North Carolina's annual average precipitation is 50 inches (127 cm), varying widely by region, with only 8.4 inches (21 cm) of snow.

Storms

Nature occasionally throws some nasty weather at North Carolina. During the spring and autumn, the coastal areas are battered by hurricanes that roar in from the Atlantic. Most residents of the Outer Banks, warned well in advance, race inland ahead of the high tides and strong winds. Only a few foolhardy folks stay behind. Mother Nature can be equally dangerous over land when tornadoes drop out of dark, overhanging clouds and whip along the countryside.

North Carolina weather is generally pleasant and temperate, allowing state residents and visitors to enjoy the outdoors and sunshine most of the time. However, it never hurts to keep an umbrella close at hand.

Hurricane Fran

In September 1996, Hurricane Fran devastated communities along the Outer Banks and swept inland, killing seventeen people. The floods and high winds caused $1 billion in damage in 80 of the state's 100 counties. Fran was one of the largest storms to pound North Carolina in the twentieth century, causing Governor Jim Hunt to call it "the worst disaster we've had in this century." In 1954, Hurricane Hazel caused considerable damage throughout the Cape Fear coast and Southport/Brunswick Islands. Then Hurricane Hugo struck in 1989 and Hurricane Andrew in 1992. These horrific storms swept away buildings, beaches, docks, boats, trees, telephone poles, and anything else that stood in their way. ■

CHAPTER SIX

Let's Take a Tour

nland from the rolling Atlantic Ocean, the wind whistles across the creeping sand dunes. The flat marshland behind the dunes is a carpet of reeds, dotted with pools of water. This was the landscape that greeted the first Europeans to visit North Carolina's Outer Banks—a string of low-lying islands off the mainland. Of course, the islands were well known to American Indians for centuries before 1524, when Giovanni da Verrazano trained his telescope on the beach.

The Native Americans and that long-ago Italian navigator would not recognize the Outer Banks on a summer afternoon today. Neither would the pirates who made their way through the channels of the Outer Banks to bury their treasure. And neither would the Confederate and Union sailors who dueled in these waters during the Civil War. Today, they would find vacationers relaxing in the sunshine, children splashing in the waves, and fishing fans casting for channel bass in the surf.

Homes in communities such as Duck are rented to tourists year-round.

Opposite: Bogue Sound near Emerald Isle

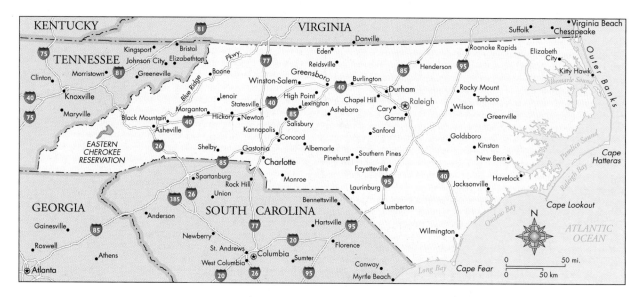

North Carolina's cities and interstates

Tourist Attractions

The crossroads villages of the Outer Banks cater to tourists during the summer months. The traffic along the highways is heavy. But in late autumn through early spring, the slow way of life returns. The towns have interesting names like Nag's Head, Kitty Hawk, and Duck. Some of the names were originally American Indian; for example, "Kitty Hawk" came from the Poteskeet word *Chickahauk*. Other towns were named for animals or early settlers. For years, the towns were mostly a collection of rambling old weathered homes, with perhaps a grocery store, gas station, church, and bait shop. A scattering of summer homes and hunting clubs dotted the sand dunes.

Typical is the Whalehead Club, a castlelike house on the far northern reaches of the Outer Banks, built in the late nineteenth century by Philadelphia millionaire Edward Knight. The club was built on the site of an old gun club that Knight purchased and tore down. He was angry because the men-only organization would not admit his wife as a member, although she was an avid hunter and

North Carolina's Nature Preserves

Environmentalists are concerned about the explosive growth of holiday homes, strip malls, and other signs of modern life along the Outer Banks because some of this expansion affects wildlife habitats.

The North Carolina National Estuarine Research Reserve is one effort by state government to preserve as much of the natural environment as possible. Several major sections of the reserve offer special habitats. The Currituck, along the Atlantic Flyway, is a major habitat for geese, falcons, ducks, gulls, swans, coots, and numerous other species. Masonboro Island, a barrier island, is home to royal terns, plovers, sandpipers, and herons. Forty-four species of fish thrive in the nearby waters.

The Rachel Carson section of the reserve is a marshy area between the mouths of the Newport and North Rivers, where many wild horses roam the dunes. Zeke's Island, in the lower Cape Fear vicinity, consists of 42 acres (17 ha) of high ground where marsh rabbits, cotton rats, gray foxes, and many birds live. Pea Island National Wildlife Refuge has more than 265 bird species in an area of more than 5,000 acres (2,000 ha). ■

an excellent shot. The new building went through a succession of owners and then stood empty until 1988, when developers purchased the surrounding property and turned the gracious structure into a restaurant and lounge. Other similar tourist attractions have sprung up along North Carolina's long coastline.

Famous Lighthouse

The famous Cape Hatteras Lighthouse at Cape Point near Buxton is one of the most photographed sites on the Outer Banks. The black-and-white striped structure is the tallest brick lighthouse in the United States. Its beacon light, towering 208 feet (64 m) above the ocean, has warned sailors about the dangerous waters since the early nineteenth century. Originally lit by flaming whale oil, the

Tourists flock to the beaches near Cape Hatteras Lighthouse.

modern light flashes an 800,000-candlepower beam every 7$\frac{1}{2}$ seconds. The light can be seen 7 miles (11 km) out to sea. When the lighthouse was originally built, it was more than 1,000 yards (1 km) from the ocean's edge. Today, with the eroding beach, the lighthouse is only 200 feet (60 m) from the water. The National Park Service is considering ways to protect the landmark.

Waterways and Bridges

Oregon Inlet opened up between the Atlantic and Pamlico Sound after a storm in 1846 and was named after the first ship that sailed through the new channel. The Bonner Bridge, across Oregon Inlet, connects the northern islands of the Outer Banks to the southern islands and has been controversial since it was built in 1964. The

The Bonner Bridge

The buildings of Brightleaf Square in Durham were tobacco warehouses at the start of the nineteenth century. At one time, 90 percent of the world's tobacco was bought and sold out of these towering brick structures. Today, the square has interesting shops, galleries, and restaurants. ■

Duke University Chapel

Duke University Chapel in Durham is designed to look like England's famous Canterbury Cathedral. It has a twenty-one-story bell tower, seventy-eight stained-glass windows, and row after row of pews. ■

massive structure obstructs some of the tidal flow, resulting in beach erosion, and dredges work constantly to keep the passage open.

Away from the tourist coast, North Carolina's pace of life slows down. Fields of tobacco and cotton and pine groves make up the Albermarle region. This is the northeast corner of the state's Coastal Plain, beginning at the Virginia border and running south to the Pamlico River. Elizabeth City, the largest community in the area, is home to 17,230 persons who make a living in the boating trade. The town is at the end of the Dismal Swamp Canal, a short-cut through the neighborhood's intercoastal waterways. The country's largest coast guard station is located here.

The Piedmont

The Piedmont is North Carolina's great plain, where its largest cities are located. Chapel Hill is fondly nicknamed "the southern part of heaven" because it is pleasantly tree-shaded and small enough to get around easily. This university center has a rich cultural life and great restaurants. Many residents come from other parts of the United States to work in research facilities nearby.

You can't miss Durham, the next stop on a trip through the Piedmont. This is a community that never slows down. Everyone seems to be rushing from office to office, from plant to plant. It is North Carolina's "city of medicine." Hospitals, clinics, laboratories, and research facilities abound. Amid the modernity, the spires, towers, and steeples of Duke University add charm to the scene. Wandering through the campus is like walking through a gothic novel. The school dates to 1838 when Quakers established Union Institute in nearby Randolph County. The rich, tobacco-growing Duke family then offered the school $100,000 if the institution admitted women and moved to Durham. The school did both—and subsequent Duke endowments helped it earn its well-deserved reputation in educational circles.

An aerial view of Durham

Raleigh is another major city in North Carolina's Research Triangle business section. It is also the state capital, with impressive wide avenues and shaded parks. However, the interior of its legislative buildings is so confusing that one guidebook advises visitors to leave a trail of popcorn so they can find their way out again. Raleigh's historic Oakwood neighborhood has more than 100 homes in gracious Victorian styles.

This is a city of museums, including the North Carolina Museum of History with its 250,000 artifacts, the North Carolina Museum of Natural Sciences, and the North Carolina Museum of Art. The latter offers more than 500 masterworks by such famous Renaissance artists as Peter Paul Rubens, Titian, and Sandro Botticelli.

Going West

Continuing southwest out of the Triangle area is Pinehurst, a small town on North Carolina's sandy central plains. In the 1880s, vacationers came to this region to relax, and Pinehurst's thirty-five championship golf courses continue to attract visitors. The town itself, with its large old houses and masses of flowers, is shaded by magnolia and dogwood trees. Pinehurst is proud of the Sir Walter Raleigh Gardens, part of the larger Sandhills Horticultural Gardens. The lovely Raleigh Gardens are modeled after a formal English garden. Just east of Pinehurst is Fayetteville, home of the Fort Bragg military post and Pope Air Force Base. The 82nd Airborne War Memorial Museum tells of the unit's missions from World War I through the Haitian crisis of the early 1990s.

Charlotte, the state's largest city, is a sea of glass and steel

The Executive Mansion

The Executive Mansion is the home of North Carolina's governor. The stately red-brick house, completed in 1891, took nine years to build. All the interior woodwork was made from trees that grow in the state's forests, and many workers on the structure were convicts who carved their initials and names on the bricks.

Governor Daniel Fowler was the first to move in, and some say he never left. According to legend, the mansion is haunted by Fowler's ghost. Subsequent governors have been awakened at night by mysterious knockings. Nobody has found a reason for the noises, despite numerous investigations.

buildings, punctuated by small parks. Charlotte began at the intersection of Trade and Tryon Streets, where two American Indian trails intersected. Scots-Irish settlers established a trading post there and built their homes in the surrounding forests.

The sixty-story Nations Bank Corporate Center is the tallest bank in the Southeast. Inside are frescoes—paintings—by Ben Long, one of the state's best-known artists. Nearby is Discovery

The 82nd Airborne War Memorial Museum at Fort Bragg

James K. Polk's Home

Ten miles (16 km) south of Charlotte is the home of James K. Polk, the eleventh president of the United States. The original log house was destroyed years ago, but visitors can walk through a replica. ■

The Queen City

Hoping to curry favor with the English colonial government, Charlotte's first residents named their little settlement after Queen Charlotte (1744–1818), wife of Britain's King George III. For this reason, one of the community's nicknames is The Queen City. ■

Place, a children's science museum that includes a recreated rain forest, a space station, and an undersea world. The Charlotte Museum of History, another enjoyable place to explore, is located in the home of Hezekiah Alexander—an early North Carolina politician. He was one of the signers of the Mecklenburg Declaration of Independence, which ended colonial rule and established the first state government.

Driving west from Charlotte takes you into higher country with forests of oak and pine. Between the towns of High Point and Hickory are many furniture factories and stores. About 60 percent of all the furniture made in the United States is built within a 200-mile (321-km) radius of this area. The Furniture Discovery Center in downtown Hickory shows the various steps taken in making furniture.

The twin towns of Winston–Salem are home to numerous theater companies, ranging from the North Carolina School for the Arts to the Piedmont Opera Theatre and the North Carolina Black Repertory Company. This region, combined with Durham and Raleigh, is America's fifth-largest urban area. More than 6 million residents live and work here. Originally full of plantations for cotton and tobacco, crops that flourished in the clay soil, the Winston–Salem vicinity was a natural business center. The tobacco still grown nearby is funneled into the R. J. Reynolds manufacturing plants, which produce 8,000 cigarettes a minute, all day, every day.

Salisbury

Founded in 1753, the historic city of Salisbury, 42 miles (67 km) northeast of Charlotte, was an important frontier town. British General Lord Cornwallis, explorer Daniel Boone, President Andrew Jackson, and other famous people stayed here over the years. The town is now best remembered as the site of one of the South's largest prison camps during the Civil War. More than 5,000 Union prisoners died and were buried here. (Shown above is Historic Hall House, *c.* 1820.) ■

Small towns and villages peek out from various secret corners in North Carolina's western mountains. The state's Scenic Byways program consists of thirty-one routes over 1,500 miles (2,400 km) of back roads. Of that total, more

than 400 miles (640 kilometers) are in the west, a scenic tour that passes waterfalls, parks, overlooks, rivers, and lakes. Everywhere along the way there are picnic sites and places to park your car and stretch your legs.

Asheville is the major town in the heart of the central mountains. One of the best views of Asheville is from Grove Park Inn's Sunset Terrace in the late afternoon. The inn is set high on a hill

Der Wachau

The Winston-Salem area was settled in the 1750s by Moravians from Germany. They purchased 100,000 acres (40,000 ha) and called the region *der Wachau*, after their leader's estate in Europe. The word *Wachau* eventually evolved into Wachovia (pronounced wa-KO-ve-a), a name now used for everything from banks to bars. ■

The Legend of the Rubies

Rubies are among the many gems found throughout the mountains of western North Carolina. According to one legend, rubies first appeared because the daughter of one American Indian leader fell in love with the son of her father's enemy. They met in secret but were discovered and put to death. Their love was so great that their blood ran together and formed the precious red stones. ■

north of town, where a visitor can see for miles. Asheville was incorporated in 1797 and named for Governor Samuel Ashe.

Scots-Irish pioneers from Northern Ireland were the first area residents, retaining an isolated rural lifestyle that contributed to a craft and folklore tradition. The railroad came through in the 1880s and opened up the area to rich city dwellers seeking a quiet, comfortable place to get away from it all. Asheville remains a jumping-off point for exploring the Blue Ridge Parkway and the region's many state and national forests.

Grove Park Inn in Asheville

CHAPTER SEVEN

North Carolina's Government

The Latin phrase *Esse quam videri* was adopted as the state motto in 1893. Translated, it means "To be, rather than to seem." These words came from the Roman politician and writer Cicero's essay on friendship. North Carolina was the only one of the original thirteen colonies not to have a motto when it became a state after the American Revolution.

The new legislative building

The state has two nicknames—the Old North State and the Tar Heel State. The first came about when the colony of Carolina was divided into north and south sections in 1712. The northern, older settlements were in what became North Carolina, hence the nickname the Old North State. The second nickname was derived from the sticky pitch, tar, and turpentine made in the colony. During the Civil War, North Carolina troops earned the nickname "Tar Heel Boys" because they "stuck it out" during fierce battles.

Rights and Rules

North Carolina's constitution has several articles that spell out how the state is to be run, and the document also affirms the basic rights of citizens. One of the most important of the thirty-five sections in Article One declares that all persons are created equal. Other sections deal with pledging allegiance to the United States, the right to a jury trail, and the separation of governmental powers.

Opposite: Historic House chamber at the state capitol in Raleigh

Article Two describes the actual governing of the state. It sets up a general assembly, consisting of a senate and a house of representatives. There are fifty state senators and a 120-member house of representatives. Both senators and representatives are elected to two-year terms, and the president of the senate is the lieutenant governor. This is an important position, because if the senate is equally divided on an issue, the president votes to break the tie.

Under its constitution, the North Carolina state government is divided into executive, legislative, and judicial branches. In 1971 and 1973, the state's Executive Organization Acts put all the agencies of the executive branch into one of seventeen departments, along with the office of governor and lieutenant governor. In 1981, community colleges were named as an eighteenth executive department.

Appointed and Elected Officials

The governor, lieutenant governor, and eight department heads are elected for four-year terms. The eight department heads are the attorney general, auditor, secretary of state, superintendent of public instruction, treasurer, and commissioners of agriculture, labor, and insurance.

Nine other department heads are appointed by the governor: administration, commerce, correction, crime control and public safety, cultural resources, environment and natural resources, health and human services, revenue, and transportation. The head of the community colleges is appointed by the State Board of Community Colleges.

North Carolina's House of Representatives in session

North Carolina's Governors

Name	Party	Term
Richard Caswell	None	1776–1780
Abner Nash	None	1780–1781
Thomas Burke	None	1781–1782
Alexander Martin	None	1782–1784
Richard Caswell	None	1784–1787
Samuel Johnston	Federalist	1787–1789
Alexander Martin	Unknown	1789–1792
R. D. Spaight Sr.	Dem.-Rep.	1792–1795
Samuel Ashe	Dem.-Rep.	1795–1798
W. R. Davie	Federalist	1798–1799
Benjamin Williams	Dem.-Rep.	1799–1802
James Turner	Dem.-Rep.	1802–1805
Nathaniel Alexander	Dem.-Rep.	1805–1807
Benjamin Williams	Dem.-Rep.	1807–1808
David Stone	Dem.-Rep.	1808–1810
Benjamin Smith	Dem.-Rep.	1810–1811
William Hawkins	Dem.-Rep.	1811–1814
William Miller	Dem.-Rep.	1814–1817
John Branch	Dem.-Rep.	1817–1820
Jesse Franklin	Dem.-Rep.	1820–1821
Gabriel Holmes	Unknown	1821–1824
H. G. Burton	Federalist	1824–1827
James Iredell Jr.	Dem.-Rep.	1827–1828
John Owen	Unknown	1828–1830
Montfort Stokes	Dem.	1830–1832
D. L. Swain	Whig	1832–1835
R. D. Spaight Jr.	Dem.	1835–1836
E. B. Dudley	Whig	1836–1841
J. M. Morehead	Whig	1841–1845
W. A. Graham	Whig	1845–1849
Charles Manly	Whig	1849–1851
D. S. Reid	Dem.	1851–1854
Warren Winslow	Dem.	1854–1855
Thomas Bragg	Dem.	1855–1859
John W. Ellis	Dem.	1859–1861
Henry T. Clark	Dem.	1861–1862
Z. B. Vance	Dem.	1862–1865
W. W. Holden (provisional governor)	Rep.	1865
Jonathan Worth	Dem.	1865–1868
W. W. Holden	Rep.	1868–1871
T. R. Caldwell	Rep.	1871–1874
C. H. Brogden	Rep.	1874–1877
Z. B. Vance	Dem.	1877–1879
T. J. Jarvis	Dem.	1879–1885
A. M. Scales	Dem.	1885–1889
D. G. Fowle	Dem.	1889–1891
Thomas M. Holt	Dem.	1891–1893
Elias Carr	Dem.	1893–1897
D. L. Russell	Rep.	1897–1901
Charles B. Aycock	Dem.	1901–1905
R. B. Glenn	Dem.	1905–1909
W. W. Kitchin	Dem.	1909–1913
Locke Craig	Dem.	1913–1917
Thomas W. Bickett	Dem.	1917–1921
Cameron Morrison	Dem.	1921–1925
Angus Wilton McLean	Dem.	1925–1929
O. Max Gardner	Dem.	1929–1933
J. C. B. Ehringhaus	Dem.	1933–1937
Clyde R. Hoey	Dem.	1937–1941
J. Melville Broughton	Dem.	1941–1945
R. Gregg Cherry	Dem.	1945–1949
W. Kerr Scott	Dem.	1949–1953
William B. Umstead	Dem.	1953–1954
Luther H. Hodges	Dem.	1954–1961
Terry Sanford	Dem.	1961–1965
Daniel K. Moore	Dem.	1965–1969
Robert W. Scott	Dem.	1969–1973
James E. Holshouser Jr.	Rep.	1973–1977
James B. Hunt Jr.	Dem.	1977–1985
James G. Martin	Rep.	1985–1993
James B. Hunt Jr.	Dem.	1993–

North Carolina's State Symbols

State beverage: Milk Milk is the official beverage of North Carolina, adopted in 1987. The state ranks twentieth among dairy-producing states in the nation, producing 179 million gallons (677 million l) of milk per year. State residents drink more than 143 million gallons (541 million l) of milk every year.

State bird: Cardinal The cardinal was selected to be the state bird in 1943. It is sometimes called the winter redbird, because it is the only scarlet bird seen during North Carolina's coldest, snowy months.

State dog: Plott hound The plott hound is the official North Carolina dog, bred in the mountains since the 1750s, and selected in 1989. It is a great tracker and was once used to hunt wild boar. The hound, which has a brindled coat and a buglelike call, was named after Jonathan Plott, who developed the breed. It is one of only four dogs known to be of American origin.

State flower: Flowering dogwood The dogwood tree is found throughout North Carolina, making its blossoms the perfect state flower. It was selected in 1941. The blossoms appear in early spring and bloom until summer. They are usually white, but lovely pink flowers appear now and then.

State gem: Emerald More than 300 kinds of minerals are found in North Carolina, more than in any other state. In 1973, the state selected the emerald as its official stone. In 1970, the largest emerald ever found in North America up to that time was found near Hiddenite. The stone was cut and polished, increasing its value to $100,000.

State insect: Honeybee The honeybee was chosen as the state's official insect in 1973.

State mammal: Gray squirrel The gray squirrel was named the state mammal in 1969.

State reptile: Eastern box turtle In 1979, the North Carolina legislature named the eastern box turtle as the state's official reptile.

State rock: Granite Granite was designated as the official rock in 1979, because the state has an abundance of it. The largest open-face granite quarry in the world lies outside Mount Airy in Surry County, measuring 1 mile (1.6 km) long and 1,800 feet (548 m) wide.

State tree: Pine The state tree is the pine, selected in 1963 because of its role in North Carolina's history.

State vegetable: Sweet potato Schoolchildren in Wilson County petitioned the state legislature in 1995 to choose the sweet potato as the state vegetable because North Carolina is the largest producer of sweet potatoes in the nation. More than 4 billion pounds (1.8 billion kg) of sweet potatoes are harvested annually.

The State Flag and Seal

The state flag was adopted in 1885. It has a blue vertical stripe on the left. In the center of the stripe is a white star, with the letter *N* on its left and the letter *C* on its right. Above the star is the date of the Mecklenburg Declaration of Independence—May 20, 1775. Below the star is the date when North Carolinians told their delegates to the Constitutional Congress to vote for independence—April 12, 1776.

The state seal, adopted in 1984, also bears these dates. The standing figure on the seal represents Liberty and the seated figure depicts Plenty. ■

North Carolina's State Song "The Old North State"

The General Assembly of 1927 adopted the song "The Old North State" as the official song of North Carolina. It is based on a traditional tune arranged by Mrs. E. E. Randolph, with words by William Gaston.

Carolina! Carolina!
Heaven's blessings attend her,
While we live, we will cherish,
*   protect and defend her.*
Tho' the scorner may sneer at
*   and witlings defame her,*
Still our hearts swell with glad-
*   ness whenever we name her.*

Hurrah! Hurrah!
The Old North State forever.
Hurrah! Hurrah!
The good Old North State.

Tho' she envies not others, their
*   merited glory,*
Say whose name stands fore-
*   most, in liberty's story.*
Tho' too true to herself e'er to
*   crouch to oppression,*
Who can yield to just rule a
*   more loyal submission.*

Hurrah! Hurrah!
The Old North State forever.
Hurrah! Hurrah!
The good Old North State.

Then let all those who love us,
Love the land that we live in,
As happy a region as on this
*   side of heaven,*
Where plenty and peace, love
*   and joy smile before us,*
Raise aloud, raise together the
*   heart-thrilling chorus.*

Hurrah! Hurrah!
The Old North State forever.
Hurrah! Hurrah!
The good Old North State.

The state court system is split into two divisions—trial and appellate. There are thirty-nine judicial districts within the district and superior trial-courts system. The appellate courts include the state's court of appeals. A chief judge and eleven associate judges are elected for eight-year terms. The North Carolina Supreme Court is the state's highest court. It consists of a chief justice and six justices, all of whom are elected for eight-year terms. Most cases are first heard in a trial court, before a judge and jury. Appellate courts hear the appeals of cases that have already been decided at the trial-court level.

Powerful Senator

On the federal level, the state has two U.S. senators. Elected in 1973 as the first Republican senator in the state since 1895, conservative

**Republican senator
Jesse Helms**

Jesse Helms became one of the country's most powerful politicians. By the mid-1990s, Helms was head of the Foreign Relations Committee and often used his position to push legislation he favored or delay legislation he was against. These tactics often angered other senators, but they seldom went against Helms's wishes because they needed his assistance in passing bills. Helms also served on the Committee on Agriculture, Nutrition, and Forestry and was a member of the Senate Rules Committee. He was the first North Carolinian and the first Republican to receive the Golden Gavel Award, given for presiding over the Senate for more than 117 hours in 1973. He received a second Golden Gavel for presiding over the Senate more than 120 hours in 1974.

County Government

Since colonial times, North Carolina's strong system of local government has been exemplified by the counties. From the beginning, the colony relied on the counties to administer local government. One of the oldest counties in North Carolina is Beaufort, incorporated in 1705. The names of many of North Carolina's counties honor colonial administrators and Revolutionary War heroes or derive from American Indian languages. Justices of the peace, who were usually wealthy property owners, served as county managers for the royal governor. After the American Revolution, the justices were still appointed by the state governor using recommendations from the general assembly. This gave legislators a great deal of power. In the early days, the justices of the peace appointed sheriffs, wardens of the poor, and other officials. They sat

North Carolina's counties

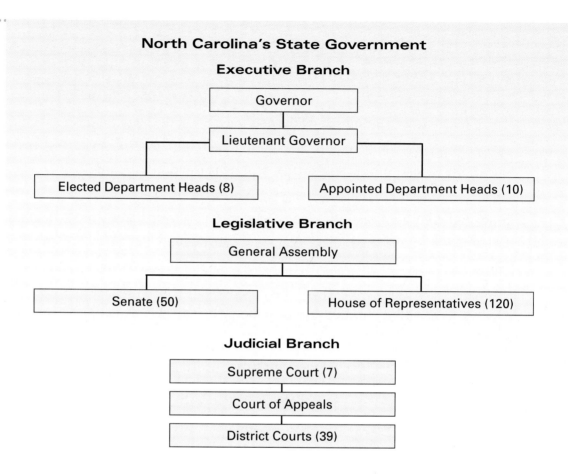

North Carolina's State Government

Executive Branch

Governor

Lieutenant Governor

Elected Department Heads (8)

Appointed Department Heads (10)

Legislative Branch

General Assembly

Senate (50)

House of Representatives (120)

Judicial Branch

Supreme Court (7)

Court of Appeals

District Courts (39)

together in a court of pleas and quarter sessions to hear civil cases. This process existed until the end of the Civil War.

When the North Carolina constitution was rewritten in 1868, its authors devised a more democratic method of governing. The old court of pleas was eliminated, judges were selected, and boards elected to manage the county's affairs. Each county was divided into townships, with the voters electing two justices of the peace and a clerk. Each township also had a constable and a school committee. This system was set up to favor the Republican Party, which took control of the state briefly during Reconstruction after

Union Square at the capitol

the Civil War. It was intended to break the power held by the landowners and merchants who had previously dominated North Carolina politics.

Control Regained

Seven years after the township system was set up, a group of conservative politicians regained control of state government. They amended several provisions in the state's new constitution that provided for election of officials by the people. Much of the power was then returned to the justices of the peace. This arrangement went on for another twenty years before the right of the people to elect county commissioners was restored. Townships then lost much of their power but were kept as convenient administrative units for road-building, maintenance, and similar local matters. In 1905, voters in all 100 counties regained direct control over their boards of commissioners.

Today, each of the state's 100 counties is governed by a board of three to seven commissioners who are elected to two- or four-year terms. The boards usually meet monthly to discuss county affairs and to allocate funds for projects ranging from bridge construction to park development. Other elected county officers include a sheriff, superior-court clerk, treasurer, and registrar of deeds. A county attorney who serves as the board's legal adviser is appointed by the board. County managers are hired or appointed.

A community in Winston-Salem

Five Hundred Municipalities

On a local level, North Carolina has more than 500 incorporated municipalities. Each community has home rule—it may amend its own charter and levy local taxes. An area with increasing population may petition the general assembly to move from unincorporated status to incorporated. Many burgeoning suburbs around major metropolitan areas have done this so that they can collect taxes to pay for local services. Most cities have a council–city manager form of government. A city manager is a professional administrator hired by the city to supervise all municipal affairs. Smaller communities usually have a mayor–city council system of management.

After Reconstruction, Democrats traditionally held most positions of political importance in North Carolina. However, Republicans have gained more prestige over the past few decades as

the state became affluent and increasing numbers of outsiders moved in. Showing the change in political focus, the Republican presidential nominee in 1928 was the only one to capture the state's votes between 1865 and 1968. Since that time, the Republican nominee has won in all the state's presidential elections except the one in 1976. In 1972, James E. Holshouser Jr. became the first Republican governor since 1896.

CHAPTER EIGHT

How North Carolina Works

I n the recent past, North Carolina was primarily an agricultural state where acres and acres of tobacco and corn stretched out to the horizon and cattle grazed in lush pastures. Now, North Carolina is better known for insurance, banking, medicine, research, and related service-sector industries. Glittering office buildings and sprawling suburbs cover what were once green fields. Busy highways cut woodlots into neatly quartered sections. The face of much of North Carolina has changed with the times, a factor accepted by the state's workforce of 3.5 million.

Tobacco being cultivated on the Duke homestead in Durham

But while it is not foremost in the state today, agriculture is still important. The state ranks among the highest in production of broilers—chickens from five to twelve weeks old. Sprawling hatcheries are a common sight in Pitt, Wilkes, Nash, and Alexander counties, while turkeys and ducks are raised in Duplin and Sampson counties, and dairy cattle dot the pastures in western North Carolina. Corn and soybeans are the principal crops in the east, with peanuts and sweet potatoes grown in the Piedmont. Raising grapes and making wine have been state traditions since colonial times.

North Carolina leads the states in making tobacco products, including about half the nation's cigarettes and much of its pipe and chewing tobacco. Factories in Greensboro, Reidsville, and

Opposite: The North Carolina National Bank

Winston–Salem turn out millions of cigarettes per day. Even with the increase of antismoking regulations, victorious lawsuits against the tobacco companies, and research showing that smoking is hazardous to health, the international use of tobacco products continues to rise. This guarantees a ready market, steady jobs, and a strong profit for the tobacco companies. The manufacturers' deep financial pockets contribute to their political clout, so few of the state's legislators are willing to press the antismoking issue.

Centuries ago, American Indians cultivated the broad, leafy tobacco plant. They used dried, crushed tobacco leaves for ceremonial and social occasions. The first Europeans to come to North America were introduced to the pungent drug and took their nicotine habit back home with them. The practice of "lighting up" or "chawing" eventually spread around the world.

North Carolina's natural resources

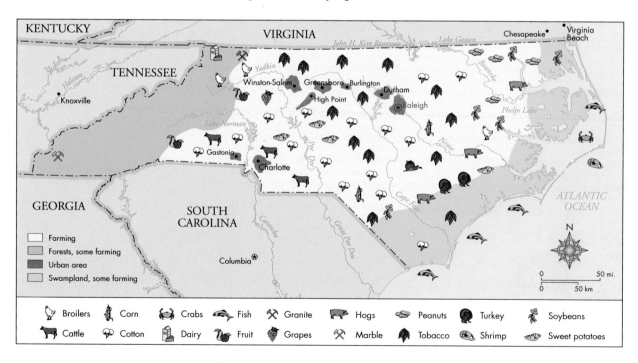

The tale of tobacco is an economic success story for North Carolina. Aggressive entrepreneurs, such as North Carolina's Duke family, made fortunes in the tobacco industry over the years. The financial empire established by Washington Duke in the 1880s is still going strong. The family's fortunes began with hard work, luck, and promise. Duke began cultivating tobacco in 1850 and hired slave labor from nearby plantation owners to help him during planting and harvesting. Although he favored the Union cause and didn't want North Carolina to break away from the United States at the outset of the Civil War, Duke was eventually conscripted into the Confederate army. After the war, he returned to farming and producing smoking tobacco. On his peddling trips around the state, he used a broken-down old wagon and two blind mules.

He helped his son Brodie establish a tobacco-manufacturing plant in Durham, which already had a reputation for producing quality tobacco for smoking and chewing. Other sons, Benjamin and James Buchanan, called "Buck," also came into the business. They started using a cigarette-making machine in 1884, cutting the cost of manufacturing in half. Previously, cigarettes were handmade by skilled laborers, often brought from Europe.

What North Carolina Grows, Manufactures, and Mines

Agriculture	Manufacturing	Mining
Tobacco	Tobacco products	Crushed stone
Chickens	Chemicals	Phosphate rock
Hogs	Furniture	
Turkeys	Textiles	
	Machinery	

James and Benjamin
Duke in Atlantic City,
New Jersey, 1920

The family then spent thousands of dollars to advertise its products, an unusual practice in the early days of the industry. Soon the Dukes surpassed their competitors. They were always looking for ways to grow as a company. In 1890, the Duke company joined forces with four of its largest rivals to form the American Tobacco Company. The resulting giant conglomerate—group of companies—now has a major share of the tobacco products manufactured in the United States.

Some of the millions of dollars earned by the Duke family went into the founding of Duke University, one of America's most prominent institutions of higher learning. Various Duke foundations also give hundreds of thousands of dollars to arts and charity organizations in North Carolina every year.

Today, industry fuels most of the state's robust growth—64 percent of the state's economic strength is now derived from industries rather than agriculture. The major companies are located in North Carolina's large metropolitan areas. Lowe's, a giant distributor of construction materials, is in Wilkesboro. Food Lion, a national grocery-store chain, operates from Salisbury. NationsBank and First Union, two huge banking companies, are headquartered in Charlotte, which has become one of America's principal financial centers. First Wachovia, another major banking firm, calls Winston–Salem its home.

Goods Produced

Manufacturing plants employ most of the state's workers, with 900,000 persons turning out everything from furniture to clothing to aluminum cans. Manufacturing makes up 29 percent of the state's gross economic output, one of the highest percentages of any state. North Carolina companies make some $60 billion worth of goods every year, from raw material to finished products.

Chemical manufacturing, another major anchor of the state's highly industrialized world, employs 48,941 persons in a variety of fields and makes up 6 percent of the total workforce. Pharmaceuticals and synthetic fibers are the leading products made in the state's three "S" cities—Southport, Salisbury, and Shelby. Kinston and Enka are home to several chemical plants, while forty-five drug companies are based in North Carolina. Other firms make detergents, plastic materials, and fertilizers.

Fabrics Made

Textile production is ranked fifth among the state's employers, with 765 firms employing 60,837 persons. Since the beginning of the 1900s, North Carolina's mills have produced many types of fabrics. Today, more than 1,200 plants turn out hosiery, denim, carpets, blouses, sheets, and towels. The value of these products has reached $5 billion a year. As a complementary business, several firms in North Carolina make specialized equipment for mills. ■

North Carolina leads all the other states in the manufacture of household items. High Point—the Furniture Capital of America—has more than 120 factories in the area making tables, chairs, desks, beds, and sofas. Other factories are situated in Thomasville, Statesville, Hickory, Lexington, and Lenoir.

Services

Personal-service companies also play an important role in North Carolina's economy. They range from medical research at Duke University in Durham to insurance and banking in Charlotte.

Government is also considered part of the state's economic mix. Several of the largest military bases in the country are located in

Research Triangle Park

In the late 1950s, North Carolina State, the University of North Carolina, and Duke University joined forces to make the Raleigh-Durham area a job hotspot, keeping native North Carolinians at home and attracting thousands of eager new employees to their research centers and laboratories.

IBM built offices in Research Triangle Park (RTP) in 1965, setting the stage for international companies to locate there. Today, firms in RTP focus on biochemicals, health care, telecommunications, computer technology, and related services. More than 35,000 North Carolinians work in RTP. ■

North Carolina. They include the Army's Fort Bragg, the Sunny Point Military Ocean Terminal, the Marines' Camp Lejeune, Cherry Point Air Station, and Seymour Johnson Air Force Base. Thousands of raw recruits and long-time veterans flood the streets of nearby towns when they are off duty. They visit restaurants, nightclubs, tourist attractions, grocery stores, and movie theaters close to the military installations, contributing to local economies.

Gas and electrical power companies keep appliances serviced in homes and industry. Two-thirds of the electric power in the state is produced locally; one-third is purchased from power companies in South Carolina. Sixty-five percent of the plants burn coal; nuclear-power plants provide another 25 percent; and hydroelectric plants provide the remaining 10 percent of the state's power needs.

Business Development

To help state businesses on an international level, the World Trade Center of North Carolina holds classes on exporting, sponsors

The Fontana Dam and hydroelectric plant

conferences on business opportunities abroad, and hosts trade delegations. The trade center is located in Charlotte. Canada is North Carolina's chief international trading partner, followed by Japan, Saudi Arabia, Mexico, and the United Kingdom. North Carolina exports totaled $17.5 billion in 1996. Industrial machinery, chemicals, and electronic gear are the biggest sellers.

The North Carolina Department of Commerce oversees business development in the state, encouraging companies to expand or to locate there. It also sponsors job training and counseling to laid-off workers or people seeking to improve their skills. In addition, the department has been working toward attracting global business. It has opened offices in Dusseldorf, Germany; Hong Kong, China; and Tokyo, Japan.

Ports and Seafood

North Carolina capitalizes on its seacoast and long oceangoing heritage. The state operates deepwater ports at Wilmington and More-

Foreign Investments

Foreign companies in North Carolina produce consumer items ranging from cookies to copper cable and cabinets, employing nearly 222,000 workers. Japanese manufacturer ASMO Company decided to come to North Carolina because local promoters paid attention to details. Japanese citizens already living in the state arranged to have local farmers grow Japanese vegetables. They also set up Japanese-language lessons for children of ASMO employees. Business people in the area were even taught the proper way to accept business cards from visiting Japanese. They were told not to jam the cards in their pockets or write on them. Both actions are seen as insults in Japan. ■

A Saudi ship docks at Wilmington port.

head City where ships from around the world dock to pick up goods transported there from around the United States. The state also leases a small harbor at Southport and truck/train terminals in Charlotte and Greensboro. The state's Ports Authority manages these facilities.

The Wanchese Seafood Industrial Park, located in Dare County, was also set up by the state to promote and support the seafood industry. The state leases sites in the park to firms that process seafood or have other marine-related operations such as boat repair. The state's annual fish catch is estimated at around $65 million. Anyone who loves seafood appreciates North Carolina blue crab and offshore clams. In addition, powerful fishing boats bring in tons of flounder and shrimp from the ocean. Trout, catfish, and even crayfish are grown at fish farms. North Carolina's natural lakes and man-made pools contribute to the growing aquaculture industry.

Business Opportunities

North Carolina has a strong minority business community in which both African-American and Native American companies play an important role. There are 603 minority-owned construction firms, 149 trucking companies, 95 financial-service firms, 44 manufacturing plants, and 292 professional-service concerns, such as dental and doctor offices, law firms, and computer-technology companies.

Since 1980, the state's film office has worked closely with production companies in finding shooting sites and referring professional crews for work in films and television. They contribute more than $400 million a year to the state economy. The *Ninja Turtles* series, the *Indiana Jones Chronicles, Richie Rich,* and portions of *Forrest Gump* were made in North Carolina. *Bandwagon,* a story about rock bands, was released in late 1997.

Tourists and Transportation

Any tourist dropping by the Chelsea Restaurant in New Bern, visiting Fort Macon State Park, or fishing in the Nantahala River helps the state's financial picture. The Commerce Department's

At Charlotte
International Trade
Center, business is
conducted year-round.

Division of Travel and Tourism promotes North Carolina to national and international visitors. In 1996, the state earned $9.6 billion from tourists, mainly through restaurants and hotels.

A strong transportation network is needed to accommodate all this business and industry. The state's Department of Transportation (DOT) is responsible for overseeing the highways, waterways, and airports in North Carolina. The DOT sponsored the nation's first Bicycling and Pedestrian Conference in Asheville in

Population of North Carolina's Major Cities (1990)	
Charlotte	469,600
Raleigh	253,200
Greensboro	203,100
Winston-Salem	169,100
Durham	146,300
Fayetteville	87,600
Jacksonville	83,400
High Point	75,000

1997. Called "Walkable Communities," it provided a forum for government, motorists, hikers, and cyclists to discuss road construction.

Airports, Waterways, and Highways

The Raleigh–Durham International Airport is used by corporate jets and major national airlines ferrying businesspeople to and from meetings. More than 10 million persons and 93,000 thousand tons of cargo pass through the airport each year.

Early settlers used the state's rivers as highways, and even now, free ferry boats make it easy to cross the Pamlico River and other waterways. State-run ferries also carry vehicles and passengers to and from harbors on the mainland to the Outer Banks.

As early as the eighteenth century, a system of roads spun out from the towns to rural areas. Today, semitrailer trucks make deliveries to most states east of the Mississippi within two days via Interstates 40, 85, and 95, and their connections. But even with today's high-speed technology and the many safety features that make travel simpler and more convenient, nature sometimes strikes back. Massive rock slides in 1997 on mountainous Interstate 40 along the Tennessee border closed this major road for several months.

Train Service

By 1840, trains were widely used, linking the state with all of its neighbors. The 161-mile (259-km) Wilmington and Raleigh line was once considered the longest in the world. Today, twenty-five rail lines provide freight and passenger service, connecting North

Trains connect North Carolina's major cities.

Biking and "Training"

A new twist on cycling through North Carolina is Amtrak's Piedmont Service, which accepts bikes that can be secured in a baggage-car luggage rack. Many cyclists use the service for overnight and weekend trips between Raleigh and Charlotte with stops in Cary, Durham, Burlington, Greensboro, High Point, Salisbury, and Kannapolis. Cyclists can hop on—or off—the train at any stop. ▪

Carolina's major cities. The North Carolina Department of Transportation is supporting construction of a high-speed rail corridor from Charlotte to Raleigh and on to Washington, D.C. Beginning in 1996, special traffic-control devices were installed at train crossings to prevent motorists from endangering their lives driving around the gates. This first step in making the corridor safe allowed the trains to travel more rapidly.

The Media

Everyone in business turns to the financial pages of the state's newspapers to find out what is happening on the financial front, as

well as to *The Wall Street Journal, Business Week,* and similar national publications. The state's first newspaper was the *North Carolina Gazette,* established in New Bern in 1751. The *Raleigh Register* put out its first edition in 1799. The *Charlotte Observer* and Raleigh's *News and Observer* are the state's major daily newspapers today. There are more than 200 other daily and weekly newspapers, plus 150 periodicals published in the state. The *Charlotte Post* has been the state's principal African-American newspaper since 1880.

One of the longest-running radio stations in the country, WBT of Charlotte, started operations in 1922. By 1949, television had made its appearance. Sets were tuned in to WBTV in Charlotte and WFMY in Greensboro. Now there are more than 308 radio stations, 40 television stations, and 20 cable stations.

North Carolina is moving toward the future, economically secure and ready for the next stage of its development.

Opposite: As North Carolina's economy improves, its financial districts expand to meet business needs.

CHAPTER NINE

North Carolina's Wonderful People Mix

The North Carolinians are a marvelous mix of races and ethnic heritages: Native American, African-American, European, Hispanic, Asian. Go to any classroom from Kitty Hawk to Maggie Valley and talk with Tom, Carlos, or Teju. Last names are just as varied— Wolfe, Yow-Jen, or Domingo. A glance through any North Carolina telephone book confirms this diversity.

A diversity of races is represented in North Carolina schools.

New Arrivals

This mix is derived from generations of arrivals from all corners of the globe, and people are still coming, lured by the opportunities for work, cultural experiences, education, and leisure activities. Typical of the state's newest citizens are New Yorker Tony Cirigliano, who now works in Raleigh for the U.S. Probation Office–Eastern District. His wife Suzette, a Californian, is a medical office worker in a local hospital. William Colby, of Milwaukee, Wisconsin, attended the University of North Carolina–Charlotte and decided to stay because he liked the city. He now sells truck engines. Professor Jamal Al-Menayes of Kuwait teaches in the School of Journalism and Mass Communications at the University of North Carolina–Chapel Hill. In 1990, there were 6.6 million state residents. By 1996, more than 7.3 million people called North Carolina their home.

Opposite: In multi-ethnic schools, students learn about the traditions of other countries from one another.

Native Americans continue to celebrate their rich traditions.

Early Settlers

The American Indians showed the first European arrivals how to survive in what looked to the newcomers like a wilderness. The Indians used the plants, water, and wildlife in harmony with nature. The European arrivals, unaccustomed to that lifestyle, suffered until they could adapt the environment to their needs.

The Spanish were the first to explore the North Carolina coast, but they were not the first settlers. Most of the earliest pioneers were English, Scots, or Irish. Many fled prison sentences in their homelands or were persuaded to come to the colony with promises of land and money. They were usually poor, glad to escape from political and religious oppression in Europe. Thousands of the original settlers who made permanent homes in North Carolina came from Virginia or colonies farther north. They carved out farms and villages after taking over the land of the Native Americans.

Typical of the early settlers were the Moravians who came to North Carolina in the late eighteenth century. Originally from Germany, these pioneers traveled along the Old Wagon Road from Pennsylvania looking for a place where they could worship in

At Old Salem, visitors experience what life was like centuries ago.

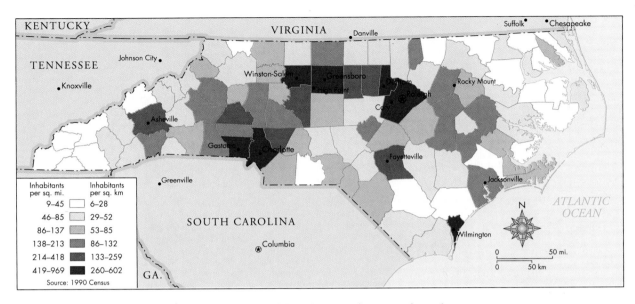

peace. One of their communities was Old Salem—about an hour's drive north of Charlotte. The community's original village has been restored and is open to tourists. Villagers in Moravian costumes describe life on the frontier.

According to tradition, married women wear tall straw hats and girls wear bonnets. A clockmaker, baker, tinsmith, and other tradespeople demonstrate their crafts in the village. The Moravian love of music is highlighted on holidays with concerts and choirs, and on Christmas Eve a town crier rings his handbell to announce the birth of Christ, just as the original Moravians did. Brass bands play during Easter sunrise services, lining a procession route from the town square to the local cemetery, which has been scrubbed and bedecked with flowers for the occasion.

Another group of Germans traveled from along the Rhine River to England and then went on to the Carolinas in the eighteenth century. They were made British citizens before being allowed to emigrate to the New World. Some settled in Pennsylvania and then moved south like the Moravians. Arriving in the

North Carolina Barbecue

Eastern North Carolinians are proud of their cider-vinegar-based barbecue sauce. The region is famous for whole-hog barbecues, where the animal is slowly cooked in a big pit and then fed to dozens of guests. This recipe is an easy approximation that can be made at home, with just part of the hog. Every North Carolinian has a favorite recipe, but the common denominator that separates North Carolina Barbecue from others is the cider-vinegar base.

Ingredients:

    2 lbs. pork shoulder roast

       bacon fat

    2 cloves of garlic, pressed

    1/2 cup ketchup

    1/4 cup apple cider vinegar

    1/4 teaspoon of sugar

    1/2 teaspoon of salt

       cayenne pepper to taste (1 or 2 teaspoons, depending on how spicy you want it)

Directions:

Preheat oven to 300°F.

Brown pork roast with the garlic in a little bacon fat, then place the roast in a Dutch oven.

Mix ketchup, vinegar, garlic, sugar, salt, and cayenne pepper in a saucepan and bring to a boil. Pour mixture over the roast and cover. Bake for about 2 hours (an hour per pound) or until the meat is starting to fall off the bone, basting occasionally with the drippings.

When the meat is done, let it cool a little, or you can store it overnight (covered) in the refrigerator. (You can heat it up in a frying pan with a little more vinegar and cayenne the next day.) When the meat has cooled enough so that it's safe to handle, pull it into bite-sized pieces. Season to taste with a little more cider vinegar and a hot sauce like Tabasco sauce.

Serve with coleslaw, corn bread, hush puppies, or french fries.

Serves 3–4 persons.

Piedmont, they found perfect land for farming. They married young and had large families, sometimes as many as thirteen children. Social life centered around their churches, which were usually Lutheran or Reformed Lutheran. Reading the Bible was a major pastime.

There were so many Germans throughout the colonies after the Revolutionary War, especially in the Carolinas, that German was seriously considered as the official language of the United States. Today, the *Deutschen Schuyle Charlotte*—a German school in Charlotte—teaches German language and culture to children as young as four.

Newcomers Prosper

In spite of all the difficulties, the South prospered. The Jeanerettes, a family who can trace their roots back to a period before the Revolutionary War, were originally French Protestants called Huguenots

The Hardships of Early North Carolina

Getting to North Carolina was very difficult in pioneer days. One immigrant described his journey from Europe aboard an old ship. He listed a few of the hardships, including "innumerable noxious odors and fumes, nausea, fevers, dysentery, headaches, oppressive heat, constipation, boils, scurvy, cancer, mouth-rot from eating salty foods, putrid water, frost, continual dampness, fleas and so many lice it was necessary to scrape them from the body." Children under seven years old seldom survived the trip.

It was rugged living on the North Carolina frontier, too. With few towns and no doctors, home remedies were often used when someone was ill or hurt. Many people did not survive illnesses and injuries that today are simply inconveniences. ■

Some North Carolina towns have restored their historic sites to promote tourism.

who fled persecution in the seventeenth century. Abraham Jeanerette, the first family member to settle in the colonies, arrived in 1720 at Charles Towne, South Carolina. As the generations evolved, the Jeanerette name popped up all over the Carolinas. Elias Jeanerette was an artillery sergeant in the colonial army and his youngest son, Samuel, fought for the Confederates in the Civil War. Wilson, one of Samuel's sons, was killed in that war. One of Samuel's great-grandsons, John Wilson Jenrette Jr., served in the U.S. Congress. Over those years, the Jeanerette name underwent many changes.

Islands Settled

North Carolina's islands were sometimes settled almost by accident. In the early eighteenth century, shipwrecked sailors settled on Ocracoke Island on the Outer Banks. They quickly adapted to their environment. They lived by fishing and looting other wrecks, and they also captured and sold wild horses. These animals are believed to have been descendants of animals left behind by Sir Richard Grenville, who stopped there on his way to colonize Roanoke Island in 1585.

African-Americans

Another major population group did not come on their own. Men, women, and children captured in Africa and brought to the Carolinas had to endure more than 200 years of slavery before gaining their freedom. But the African-Americans emerged strong and proud from that terrible era of slavery. Starting with nothing, they made a place for themselves in their new free world. As an example, Durham's Reverend Edian Markham stuck four posts in the ground in 1868, made a roof of branches, and called his congregation together. St. Joseph's Church, now one of the South's most beautiful Victorian brick buildings, traces its origin back to those humble beginnings.

One of the men who helped construct the church was Robert B. Fitzgerald, an African-American entrepreneur who came to

Commercial crabbing on Ocracoke Island

Durham from Pennsylvania in 1865. Fitzgerald's brickworks were famous throughout the area for their quality, so it was natural they would be used for St. Joseph's Church. Fitzgerald eventually became the first president of the Mechanics and Farmers Bank, established in 1907.

Course of Study

Since 1898, North Carolina has had a standard course of study in which all public school students supposedly were taught the same skills—reading, writing, science, arts, and arithmetic. Until the 1960s, however, black students and white students attended separate schools. The schools were supposed to be equal, but lack of money for African-American schools meant that black youngsters were often denied equal access to quality education. Finally, desegregation opened the doors to better opportunities for everyone. In

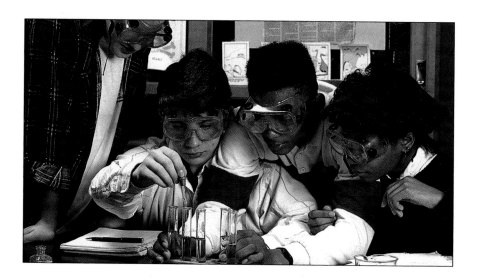

Today, North Carolina schools provide equal opportunity for all their students.

Roll Call

There are 1,570 elementary schools and 308 secondary schools in North Carolina, and the ethnic distribution of the pupils reflects the diversity of the state. In 1996, 769,065 white pupils represented 64.1 percent of the school population. African-Americans made up 30.7 percent, with 368,478 pupils. Next came Hispanics, at 2.3 percent (27,300 pupils), Native Americans at 1.5 percent (18,092), and Asians at 1.4 percent (17,520 pupils). Many of the students are bused to school, especially in rural counties.

Numerous private schools are affiliated with a religious denomination, such as Catholic, Lutheran, or Baptist. The Carolina Agency for Jewish Education holds many educational programs around the state in synagogues and sponsors outreach programs to non-Jewish North Carolinians. ■

Regional Speech

While regional speech patterns become more and more blurred in the age of national television, pockets of different pronunciations can be found in North Carolina. For instance, the following can still be heard in the state's mountainous west:

skeerce	scarce
laig	leg
onct	once
deef	deaf
yaller	yellow
ketch	catch
bar'l	barrel
hit	it
goom	gum

Some things have different names in various parts of the state. In the Blue Ridge Mountains, a bag is a "poke" and in the Piedmont flatlands, it's a "sack." Along the seacoast, people use words you won't hear anywhere else. A "bloater" is a fat person, a "may" is a sweetheart, and "to scoop" is to run away. Inland, a highchair is a "high-bob," a "shoe-round" is a dance, "us-all" means "me," and "ya-all" refers to "you." And when a tobacco-field worker "sees monkeys" it means that he is overcome by heat. ■

A high-school shop
class in industrial arts

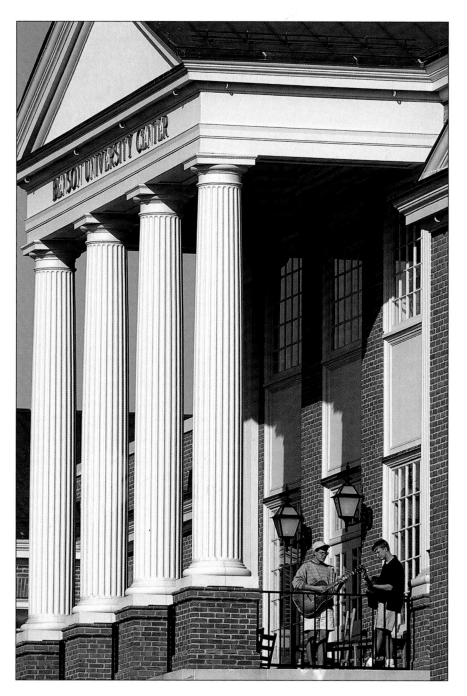

Students relaxing at
Lake Forest University

1985, the state's school system developed the Basic Education Program, an updated series of courses that better meets the needs of modern North Carolina and prepares its young people for a rapidly changing world.

Higher Learning

Many North Carolina students go on to higher education after graduating from high school. They may attend classes at public or private four-year colleges, two-year colleges, or vocational schools. The state's community-college system is the third largest in the United States. Each year, the system's fifty-eight facilities enroll 500,000 students. There are also eighteen industrial-education centers that cater to students who want to learn auto mechanics, carpentry, plumbing, bricklaying, and other trades.

The University of North Carolina is made up of sixteen institutions in Charlotte and other cities. The first campus in Chapel Hill was chartered in 1789 and opened its doors in 1795—making it the first such school in the United States.

Private higher education can trace its beginnings back to 1772 and the founding of Salem College, one of the first colleges in America for women. The second-oldest college in the state is Louisburg College, founded in 1787. By 1877, there were twenty private colleges in North Carolina, and today thirty-seven are accredited by the Southern Association of Colleges and Schools. They are affiliated with fourteen religious denominations and enroll more than 50,000 students. One-third of all the bachelor's degrees awarded in North Carolina each year are earned by students of these schools.

CHAPTER TEN

Athletes, Artists, and Actors

From sports to the arts, North Carolina seems to exert a certain power. Basketball great Michael Jordan leaps high from the dotted line, gracefully dunking the ball behind his head. The fans cheer as the Chicago Bulls' star fakes out another unsuspecting opponent. No doubt Jordan perfected that trick while attending the University of North Carolina–Chapel Hill. Author Thomas Wolfe also attended Chapel Hill, but that was several generations earlier, when Wolfe was only fifteen. The Asheville-born novelist is well known for his many books, starting with *Look Homeward, Angel* in 1929.

Noted Authors

Other noted authors who came out of North Carolina include Clyde Edgerton, who touches on his state roots in *Where Trouble Sleeps* (1997). Stretching back into the past, William Sydney Porter, known as O. Henry, was born in Greensboro in 1862 and became the nation's most widely read author in the early twentieth century. Two of his stories, "A Black Bargainer" and "Let Me Feel Your Pulse," were about North Carolina.

North Carolina's writers' community publishes an electronic magazine on the Internet, featuring artwork, short stories, and poems by the state's up-and-coming artists, authors, and poets. Among the regular contributors is illustrator Tommy Beaver, who

A statue of author O. Henry in Greensboro

Opposite: Basketball legend Michael Jordan attended college in North Carolina.

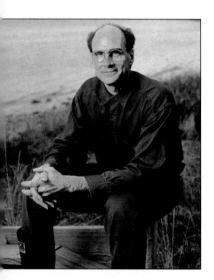

Singer James Taylor

Actor Andy Griffith on the set of the ever-popular *Mayberry RFD* television show

lives in Greensboro with his wife, Kelcie. Another is writer Tom Lanier, a union official who also writes award-winning, hard-hitting tales like *Uncle Daddy* and *The Wasteland,* stories about workers struggling for their rights. Barbara Presnell of Salisbury has published numerous short stories in many literary magazines. She teaches writing and literature at Catawba College.

Popular Musicians

Music in North Carolina ranges from drum and bugle corps to symphony orchestras. Popular musicians include songwriter, singer, and band leader George Clinton, who took the stage name of Doctor Funkenstein. His rhythms and scores changed the face of music during the 1970s. Jazz pianist Thelonious Monk was born in Rocky Mount in 1918. Other famous entertainers are singers James Taylor and Roberta Flack, bandleader Kay Kyser, country performer Ronnie Milsap, opera star Carol Brice, and gospel singer Shirley Caesar. And anybody wanting to hear good down-home, slam-bang rock and roll will enjoy Shiloh, a band from Raleigh, and Ben Folds Five, a trio from Chapel Hill.

Famous Stars

Several famous film and TV stars also call North Carolina their home. One of the best known is actor Andy Griffith. His hometown of Mount Airy has an Andy Griffith Museum. The streets of Mount Airy recalls the fictional town of "Mayberry" portrayed on the long-running TV programs *The Andy Griffith Show* and *Mayberry RFD.* Francis Bavier, the woman who played Aunt Bea on those shows, was also from North Carolina.

Other stars include the beautiful movie actress Ava Gardner, born in Smithfield. African-American actress Pam Grier was born in Winston-Salem in 1949. She starred in many adventure films. Grier most recently performed in the alien shoot-'em-up *Mars Attacks!* (1996) and *Jackie Brown* (1997). George Grizzard is also well known. Born in 1928, the Roanoke Rapids native appeared in dozens of television programs such as the miniseries "Scarlett" in 1994 and numerous films.

The Theater

North Carolina's many theater companies are a great proving ground for young performers. "Catch the Vision" is the slogan for the young people at the Hayti Heritage Center in Durham, which promotes the rich heritage and art of the community's African-Americans. The center's dance studio, performance hall, and classrooms make it a hub for the neighborhood. In addition to cultivating young talent, the center hosts touring companies such as the Black Theater Festival of Winston-Salem and the Schomburg Center in New York.

Charlotte's Theater Scene

The Children's Theater of Charlotte presents drama for youngsters from three years old to eighteen. Mainstage shows are put by on the resident troupe, while Second Stage presentations are put on by the youngsters themselves. The Children's Theater also holds workshops and seminars for teachers and students.

The Spirit Square Center for the Arts, also in Charlotte, offers drama classes for children. In addition to its three theaters, the facility has a gallery for young artists. Student actors enjoy classes at the Raleigh Little Theater and the Academy Foundation in Hampstead. ∎

Sports Hall of Fame

Michael Jordan is not the only sports hero to come from North Carolina. The state's Sports Hall of Fame has 150 inductees, ranging from pro-football player Charlie Sanders to basketball star and sportswriter Charles Harville. Each year, additional major athletes are brought into the honored circle. The Hall of Fame is located in the North Carolina Museum of History in Raleigh.

A Passion for Basketball

The central sports passion in North Carolina is basketball, and the state's college basketball programs are the center of the hoops universe. Four of the Atlantic Coast Conference's leading basketball powers are located in North Carolina: the University of North Carolina (UNC), Duke University, North Carolina State University, and Wake Forest University. Among them, UNC, Duke, and North Carolina have won seven NCAA championships (and were runners-up eight other times).

The rivalry between the UNC Tar Heels and the Duke Blue Devils ranks among the most legendary in sports. Beginning in the early 1980s, Coach Dean Smith maintained UNC as a contender for the NCAA championship almost every year (winning the title twice). Then in the late 1980s, Duke emerged as an equally potent power behind Coach Mike Kryzewski, winning back-to-back NCAA championships in 1991 and 1992. Regular-season games between UNC and Duke are passionate, all-out wars.

The Tar Heel state's love of basketball led to the state's being awarded its first major-league sports franchise in 1987, when the Charlotte Hornets joined the National Basketball Association.

Dean Smith

Considered the greatest basketball coach of the late twentieth century, Dean Smith guided the North Carolina Tar Heels for thirty-six seasons, retiring in 1997. His teams had an all-time record of 879-254, giving him more wins than any coach in college basketball history. Smith was inducted into the Basketball Hall of Fame in 1983. ■

After a few rough seasons, the Hornets quickly moved up in the standings and today are a perennial play-off contender.

Room for Football, Too

In 1995, the Carolina Panthers became the second big-time pro sports team in the state, joining the National Football League (NFL) as an expansion team. Actually, the Panthers are a team that both North and South Carolina can call their own. The team played its first season at Clemson Memorial Stadium in South Carolina. Then, in 1996, it moved to brand-new, 73,000-seat Ericsson Stadium in Charlotte, North Carolina. The Panthers felt right at home, because in just their second season, they dominated the NFL and shocked football fans around the country by winning their division. They nearly made it all the way to the Super Bowl before losing the NFC championship game to the eventual Super Bowl champs, the Green Bay Packers.

Andrea Stinson of the Charlotte Sting, one of six teams in the new Women's National Basketball Association

High School Sports and "Seniors"

For high-schoolers, the state Amateur Athletic Association baseball championships draw thousands of supporters every year. About 140 teams compete in eastern and western regionals, with the finals held in Greensboro.

"Oldsters" compete every year in the North Carolina Senior Games. The finals are held in Raleigh. The 2,500 participants—

fifty-five years or older—demonstrate that age doesn't mean a thing when it comes to staying in tip-top shape. Archery, track, swimming, table tennis, race walking, cycling, and shuffleboard are among the events.

Racing

Many other mainline sports are popular in North Carolina. A fan can find a soccer ball, sandlot volley ball, or bowling ball just about anywhere. And there's more—the roar of engines at the Charlotte Motor Speedway and the thunder of hooves as Thoroughbreds race along the stretch at the Charlotte Steeplechase Spring Race Meet. And the 570 members of the North Carolina Running Club take on all comers at marathons across the country.

Nonprofessional Sports

Many other nonprofessional pastimes are enjoyed by North Carolinians. Whitewater rafting, rock climbing, and mountain biking are only a few of the state's outdoor adventures. Avon, on Hatteras Island, is a center for windsurfing because of the steady wind blowing in from the Atlantic. Thousands of windsurfers from around the world flock to Avon during the spring and autumn, when the best breezes blow. Nearby Buxton, just south of Avon, is also a popular locale. The colorful, striped sails on the boards provide vibrant flashes of color as the surfers dash across the roaring surf. At Kitty Hawk Kites throughout the summer, instructors teach hang gliding. It is amazing to know that today's gliders fly higher and longer than did the Wright brothers in their first airplane.

Fishing is one of the most popular sports in North Carolina, whether it's bass fishing on inland streams or "going for the big ones" along the coast.

Oregon Inlet is the hub of the Outer Banks charter fishing fleet, where more than thirty boats take enthusiastic anglers out for mullet and sea bass. King mackerel, blue and white marlin, and tarpon are other fighting fish in the rolling offshore waters.

Clearly, North Carolina is a state that offers much. For residents and visitors alike, the range of geographical diversity, history, and natural beauty are abundant and exceptionally rewarding.

Whitewater rafting on the Nantahala River

Timeline

United States History

1607 The first permanent British settlement is established in North America at Jamestown.

1620 Pilgrims found Plymouth Colony, the second permanent British settlement.

1776 America declares its independence from England.

1783 Treaty of Paris officially ends the Revolutionary War in America.

1787 U.S. Constitution is written.

1803 Louisiana Purchase almost doubles the size of the United States.

North Carolina State History

1524 Giovanni da Verrazano explores the North Carolina coast.

1585 Roanoke Island is the first European attempt to settle North America.

1587 Virginia Dare is the first child of European heritage born in America.

1663 Charles II grants Carolina to eight English lords.

1712 North Carolina and South Carolina become separate colonies.

1729 North Carolina becomes a royal colony.

1768 Colonists called the Regulators organize to resist "unjust" taxes.

1771 The Regulators clash with the militia in the Battle of Alamance Creek.

1775 North Carolina becomes the first colony to declare its complete independence from Britain.

1789 North Carolina ratifies the U.S. Constitution, becoming the twelfth state to enter the union.

1792 The state capital is moved to Raleigh.

United States History

U.S and Britain **1812-15** fight the War of 1812.

The North and South fight **1861-65** each other in the American Civil War.

The United States is **1917-18** involved in World War I.

Stock market crashes, plunging the **1929** United States into the Great Depression.

The United States **1941-45** fights in World War II.

The United States becomes a **1945** charter member of the United Nations.

The United States **1951-53** fights in the Korean War.

The U.S. Congress enacts a series of **1964** groundbreaking civil rights laws.

The United States **1964-73** engages in the Vietnam War.

The United States and other nations **1991** fight the brief PersianGulf War against Iraq.

North Carolina State History

1861 North Carolina joins the Confederacy.

1868 North Carolina is readmitted to the Union under a new constitution.

1903 Wright brothers complete the first successful powered airplane flight at Kitty Hawk.

1933 North Carolina takes over support of public schools.

1950 Great industrial expansion begins.

1960 The "sit-in" movement for African-American civil rights begins in Greenboro.

1971 A new state constitution goes into effect.

1972 North Carolina elects a Republican governor and U.S. Senator for the first time in the twentieth century.

1992 Eva Clayton is elected to the U.S. House of Representatives as the first black member from North Carolina since 1901.

Fast Facts

Historic House chamber

Cardinal

Statehood date	November 21, 1789, the 12th state
Origin of state name	Named for King Charles I (Carolus in Latin) in a land grant given to Sir Robert Heath
State capital	Raleigh
State nicknames	Tar Heel State, Old North State
State motto	*Esse quam videri* (To be, rather than to seem)
State beverage	Milk
State bird	Cardinal
State dog	Plott hound
State flower	Flowering dogwood
State gem	Emerald
State insect	Honeybee

Sweet potatoes

Schoolchildren

Cape Fear

State mammal	Gray squirrel
State reptile	Eastern box turtle
State rock	Granite
State song	"The Old North State"
State tree	Pine
State vegetable	Sweet potato
State fair	Raleigh (mid-October)
Total area; rank	52,672 sq. mi. (136,420 sq km); 29th
Land; rank	48,718 sq. mi. (126,179 sq km); 29th
Water; rank	3,954 sq. mi. (10,241 sq km); 10th
***Inland water*; rank**	3,954 sq. mi. (10,241 sq km); 6th
Geographic center	Chatham, 10 mi. (16 km) northwest of Sanford
Latitude and longitude	North Carolina is located approximately between 33° 52' and 36° 34' N and 75° 27' and 84° 20' W.
Highest point	Mount Mitchell, 6,684 feet (2,037 m)
Lowest point	Sea level along the Atlantic coast
Largest city	Charlotte
Number of counties	100
Longest river	Cape Fear River, 200 miles (320 km)
Population; rank	6,657,630 (1990 census); 10th
Density	126 persons per sq. mi. (49 per sq km)
Population distribution	50% urban, 50% rural

The Blue Ridge
Parkway

Ethnic distribution (does not equal 100%)	White	75.56%
	African-American	21.97%
	Hispanic	1.16%
	Asian and Pacific Islanders	0.79%
	Other	0.48%
	Native American	0.21%
Record high temperature	109°F (43°C) at Albemarle on July 28, 1940	
Record low temperature	−29°F (−34°C) at Mount Mitchell on January 30, 1966	
Average July temperature	70°F (21°C)	
Average January temperature	41°F (5°C)	
Average yearly precipitation	50 inches (127 cm)	

Cape Lookout

North Carolina's Natural Areas

National Park

Great Smoky Mountains National Park is one of North Carolina's best-known attractions and sits on the North Carolina–Tennessee border and covers more than 521,000 acres (210,842 ha).

National Seashores

Cape Hatteras National Seashore has the tallest lighthouse in North America at 208 feet (64 m).

Cape Lookout National Seashore preserves the undeveloped Barrier Islands along the lower Outer Banks.

Nantahala National
Forest

National Historical Sites

Carl Sandburg Home National Historic Site preserves the author's home and farm.

Fort Raleigh is the site of the first attempted English settlement in North America.

National Forests

Pisgah, *Nantahala*, *Uwharrie*, and *Croatan National Forests* cover more than 1.2 million acres (486,000 ha).

State Parks

North Carolina has 63 state parks. *Kerr Lake State Recreational Area* is the largest at 106,864 acres (43,246 ha). The state also operates six educational forests designed to teach the public about the forest and its environment.

Sport Teams

NCAA Teams (Division 1)

Appalachian State University Mountaineers

Campbell University Fighting Camels

Davidson College Wildcats

Duke University Blue Devils

East Carolina University Pirates

North Carolina A&T State University Aggies

North Carolina University Wolfpack

University of North Carolina–Asheville Bulldogs

University of North Carolina–Chapel Hill Tar Heels

University of North Carolina–Charlotte 49ers

University of North Carolina–Greensboro Spartans

University of North Carolina–Wilmington Seahawks

Andrea Stinson of the
Charlotte Sting

Wake Forest University Demon Deacons

Western Carolina University Catamounts

National Basketball Association
Charlotte Hornets

National Football League
Carolina Panthers

Women's National Basketball Association
Charlotte Sting

The 82nd Airborne War Memorial Museum at Fort Bragg

Cultural Institutions

Libraries

Duke University Library and the *University of North Carolina–Durham* have the largest library collections in the state.

The North Carolina State Library and *The State Department of Archives and History* both hold significant collections on state history.

Museums

The North Carolina Museum of Art (Raleigh) is the only art museum in the United States started with state funding.

William Hayes Ackland Memorial Art Center (Chapel Hill) and the *Weatherspoon Art Gallery* (Greensboro) are important museums within the University of North Carolina system.

The Greensboro Historical Museum and the *North Carolina Museum of History* (Raleigh) have extensive collections relating to the state's history.

Performing Arts

North Carolina has one major opera company, three major symphony orchestras, and two major dance companies.

The North Carolina Dance Theater

Grandfather Mountain

Emerald Isle

Universities and Colleges

In the mid-1990s, North Carolina had seventy-five public and forty-seven private institutions of higher learning.

Annual Events

January–March

Field Trials in Pinehurst (January)

Christmas at the Homestead in Boone (January)

Camellia Show in Wilmington (February)

Horse Trials in Tryon (March)

Moravian Easter Service in Old Salem (March or April)

April–June

Festival of Flowers at Biltmore Estate in Asheville (April)

Azalea Festival in Wilmington (April)

Stoneybrook Steeplechase in Southern Pines (April)

Shad Festival in Grifton (April)

Ole Time Fiddler's and Bluegrass Festival in Union Grove (May)

Annual Emerald Isle Beach Music Festival in Emerald Isle (May)

National Hollerin' Contest in Spivey's Corner near Fayetteville (June)

Summer Festival of Music in Brevard (June–August)

Singing on the Mountain at Grandfather Mountain near Linville (June)

Rhododendron Festival in the Bakersville area (June)

The Lost Colony Outdoor Drama at Manteo (June–August)

July–September

Western North Carolina Wagon Train in Brevard (July)

Dance festivals are held annually at Town Creek Indian Mound.

Bele Chere Festival in Asheville (July)

Highland Games and Gathering of Scottish Clans at Grandfather Mountain (July)

Mountain Dance and Folk Festival in Asheville (August)

Annual Mount Mitchell Crafts Fair in Burnsville (August)

State Championship Horse Show in Raleigh (September)

Mule Days Celebration in Benson (September)

October–December

State Fair in Raleigh (October)

National 500 Auto Race in Concord (October)

Surf Fishing Tournament in Nags Head (October)

Anniversary of First Powered Airplane Flight at Kill Devil Hill (December 17)

Christmas at Biltmore in Asheville (December)

Candlelight Christmas Tour of Historic Oakwood in Raleigh (December)

Roberta Flack

Famous People

Avery Brundage (1887–1975)	Businessperson and sportsperson
Thomas Hart Benton (1782–1858)	Statesman
Thomas Lanier Clingman (1812–1897)	Soldier and statesman
James Buchanan Duke (1856–1925)	Industrialist
Roberta Flack (1940–)	Singer
Billy Graham (1918–)	Evangelist
Jesse Jackson (1941–)	Civil rights leader
Andrew Johnson (1808–1875)	U.S. president
Michael Jordan (1963–)	Basketball player

O. Henry

Dolley Madison (1768–1849)	U.S. First Lady
Thelonious Monk (1920–1981)	Jazz pianist
Edward R. Murrow (1908–1965)	Journalist and broadcaster
James Knox Polk (1795–1849)	U.S. president
William Sydney Porter [O. Henry] (1862–1910)	Author
Zebulon Baird Vance (1830–1894)	Lawyer and politician
Thomas Wolfe (1900–1938)	Author

To Find Out More

History

- Aylesworth, Thomas G., and Virginia L. Aylesworth. *Lower Atlantic: North Carolina, South Carolina.* New York: Chelsea House, 1995.

- Fradin, Dennis. *North Carolina.* Chicago: Childrens Press, 1994.

- Fradin, Dennis. *North Carolina Colony.* Chicago: Childrens Press, 1991.

- Schulz, Andrea. *North Carolina.* Minneapolis: Lerner Publications, 1993.

- Thompson, Kathleen. *North Carolina.* Austin, Tex.: Raintree/Steck-Vaughn, 1996.

Fiction

- Forrester, Sandra. *My Home Is Over Jordan.* New York: Lodestar Books, 1997.

- Houston, Gloria. *Littlejim.* New York: Beech Tree Books, 1993.

Folktales

- Chase, Richard, and Berkeley Williams Jr. *The Jack Tales.* Boston: Houghton Mifflin, 1993.

Websites

- **State of North Carolina**
  http://www.sips.state.nc.us/nchome.html
  Official website for North Carolina state government

- **North Carolina Encyclopedia**
  http://statelibrary.dcr.state.nc.us/NC/COVER.HTM
  Maintained by the state library, this site contains extensive information on North Carolina history and government.

Addresses

- **Department of Commerce**
  Travel and Tourism Division
  430 North Salisbury Street
  Raleigh, NC 27611
  Provides information on North Carolina state tourism.

- **Secretary of State**
  Publications Division
  300 North Salisbury Street
  Raleigh, NC 27611
  Provides information on North Carolina state government.

- **School Information Program**
  Travel and Tourism Division
  430 North Salisbury Street
  Raleigh, NC 27611
  Provides information on North Carolina state history.

Index

Page numbers in *italics* indicate illustrations.

Meet the Authors

Martin Hintz (left) is a professional journalist and member of the Society of American Travel Writers who has covered news-breaking events around the world. He has written numerous books in both the America the Beautiful and Enchantment of the World series. Additionally, he is the author of hundreds of magazine and newspaper travel stories.

Stephen Hintz (opposite), Martin's son and twenty-two years old at the time of writing *North Carolina,* attended his freshman and sophomore years at the University of North Carolina–Charlotte. He and his friends spent their free time exploring the state's many attractions. In 1995, Steve transferred to the University of Wisconsin–Milwaukee to complete a degree in sociology and African-American studies. In addition to his writing, Steve is an administrative assistant of Horizon House, a rehabilitation center for women recently released from jail. He is also working on a novel.

Working as a team, Martin took the research and notes provided by Steve and put them in copy form. Steve then reviewed the manuscript and adjusted the material as needed, using his experience from living and studying in North Carolina. Together they interviewed numerous North Carolinians, researched on the World Wide Web, and utilized library resources. The state government and organizations in North Carolina also provided helpful brochures and books.

Martin and Stephen are also the coauthors of *The Bahamas* (Children's Press, 1997) and two editions of the prizewinning *Wisconsin Family Guide* (Globe Pequot, 1995 and 1998).

Photo Credits